Poetry against *Torture*

Criticism, History, and the Human

Paul A. Bové

香港大學出版社

HONG KONG UNIVERSITY PRESS

Hong Kong University Press
14/F Hing Wai Centre
7 Tin Wan Praya Road
Aberdeen
Hong Kong

© Hong Kong University Press 2008

ISBN 978-962-209-926-5 (Hardback)
ISBN 978-962-209-927-2 (Paperback)

Secure On-line Ordering
http://www.hkupress.org

British Library Cataloguing-in-Publication Data
A catalogue copy for this book is available from the British Library

Printed and bound by Liang Yu Printing Factory Co. Ltd., in Hong Kong, China

Hong Kong University Press is honoured that Xu Bing, whose art explores the
complex themes of language across cultures, has written the Press's name in his
Square Word Calligraphy. This signals our commitment to cross-cultural thinking
and the distinctive nature of our English-language books published in China.

"At first glance, Square Word Calligraphy appears to be nothing more unusual
than Chinese characters, but in fact it is a new way of rendering English words
in the format of a square so they resemble Chinese characters. Chinese viewers
expect to be able to read Square Word Calligraphy but cannot. Western viewers,
however are surprised to find they can read it. Delight erupts when meaning is
unexpectedly revealed."

— Britta Erickson, *The Art of Xu Bing*

Contents

Acknowledgements

I want to thank Professor Q.S. Tong of the English Department of the University of Hong Kong for initiating the processes that allowed me to deliver these lectures over the course of several weeks during February and March, 2006. At every moment, he has been a friend, an interlocutor, and a guide who made my time in Hong Kong pleasurable and challenging. His constant care and generous talk embody the virtues of a great character and a long and life-enhancing culture.

Thanks also go to Professor Kam Louie, Dean of the Faculty of Arts, who made possible my visit and who shared his time and insights with me about education in Hong Kong and China.

The English Department of the University provided me with a fine place to work, with students to meet, and a collegial context for the exchange of ideas that I thought rare for its combination of excellence and comradery. I thank them for allowing me to join their weekly seminars and to share some of my thoughts on John Milton in America. The staff of the department facilitated all my activities and I want to thank them heartily.

Among the many excellent friends I made in Hong Kong, special thanks must go to Chris Hutton, who was Head of Department while I was there, and made me feel welcome beyond all reasonable need. Bill Ashcroft shared his experiences of Hong Kong and Australia with me; I was pleased to hear two of his talks while there. Elaine Yee Lin Ho and Douglas Kerr define the professional, historical, and social spirit of Hong Kong and embody the best of cosmopolitanism among academics. To all the others who gave so generously of their time and custom, I say thanks.

Ms. Julia Chan acted as my research assistant in Hong Kong and she more often than not ably guided me through all the differences between the University of Hong Kong and American universities. We had innumerable valuable conversations about Hong Kong culture and her research into postmodern fiction. I miss those times even now.

Ms. Ruth Hung, a graduate of the University of Hong Kong and doctoral student at Oxford, shared her knowledge of the city and Chinese intellectuals. I learned a great deal.

Finally, I must acknowledge the post-graduate students of the University who listened to me talk, who posed hard questions, and who often met informally with me during our Monday discussions. They were a new and shaping audience for me.

As always, I must express the deepest intellectual debt to my editorial colleagues at *boundary 2*, who create an environment of debate, learning, and criticism that I believe is unique. Q.S. Tong and I talked a very great deal in Hong Kong about what I was doing, about what criticism now needs to do, and about the difficult importance of U.S./China exchanges that rest on testimony of how the world looks from different places. He taught me a great deal about Chinese poetry, painting, and calligraphy that form part of the background of these pages. At the same time, being the excellent scholar of nineteenth-century Britain that he is, he saved me from an embarrassment or two about Ruskin and Keats.

Several other members of the *boundary 2* group offered me specific advice and I want to acknowledge them and apologize for taking their advice less often than I should. Joseph Buttigieg, Marcia Landy, Ronald Judy, and Dan O'Hara read lectures in various forms. Chris Connery, Wlad Godzich, and Rob Wilson allowed me to repeat the Empson materials at the University of California, Santa Cruz. That context taught me a great deal. Lindsay Waters also read the Empson materials and encouraged me to continue. Special thanks to Bruce Robbins who helped me decide on the final title for these talks. Many of the others not named here have been interlocutors for varying lengths of time. For example, while I have admired and worked with Jonathan Arac for three decades, I have come to know Tony Bogues more recently. But with all the other distinguished members of this unique collective — Don Pease, Michael Hays, Gayatri Spivak, Hortense Spillers, Aamir Mufti, and especially William Spanos — they create a density of argument and thought that nourishes and trains. Readers will feel the undying presence of Edward W. Said's honorable passion, well-chosen erudition, and path-breaking illumination throughout these pages.

Special thanks to N. John Cooper, Dean of the School of Arts and Sciences, University of Pittsburgh, who made it possible for me to be away for nine weeks during the school year. Thanks, too, to Professor David Bartholomae, Chair of

English at Pitt, who facilitated the arrangements. This is the time to express deep admiration for Dave's skills and generosity as chair as well as for his personal support. A special thanks to Professor Eric O. Clarke, a *boundary 2* as well as Pittsburgh colleague, who shared a seminar with me in the spring of 2006.

I wish to thank my friend and colleague, Meg Havran, whose generosity and skill deserve the greatest recognition. Joshua Schriftman helped me with preparing this manuscript and correcting proofs.

My doctoral students at Pittsburgh have no direct experience of these talks, but their imprint is everywhere in them. If I have a ruling motive for writing these lectures, it is to try to serve their interests in whatever way is possible — while listening as much as possible to know what their needs are and to discover the truths they share.

Carol and Laura Mastrangelo Bové supported me throughout. They made it possible for me to leave home for more than two months and they offered considerable support and love at a distance. They have tolerated my distraction in rewriting these pages over the last months. Laura provides the inspiration of a young intellectual forming herself with a commitment to thought and justice. Carol, as always, encourages me to do only what I think important, to simplify my commitments to those that matter, and to keep my prose accessible. I would get nothing done without the frisson of our endless talk about fundamental matters.

Preface

This book would never have been written had I not been honored with an invitation to lecture at the University of Hong Kong on Foundations of Euro-American Critical Theory. In searching about for a way to approach this intimidating topic, it seemed to me imperative that I couple two lines of approach, or if you will, adopt two congruent subjects. I had to choose a starting point that would set me along a path through the vast body of writing, culture, and thinking that lay about me as the field for my work. In so doing, I had to admit that I was choosing because of what I thought was best in forming modern critical practice rather than merely the theoretical aspects of the field. The field of criticism lays there crisscrossed so densely by all the same forces and creations of Western history as any other field of cultural knowledge, that to write the story of its foundations and their emergence would be an impossible task if I were to try to be complete and exhaustive.

As I expected, my topic grew before me and I soon realized that I was in the position of a Beckett character, crawling on a well-known terrain that nonetheless surprises, bogs one down, and demands constant attention. I knew that I would be speaking in what had been until recently a colonial institution where the British models of teaching and the British narratives of literary criticism and history were dominant. I knew I faced an unusual and provocative opportunity as an American in such a context. I was not only an avatar of the current imperial power and so could speak, presumably, from a universal rather than parochial position, but also I would be speaking inside one of the privileged portals of communication and exchange between the United States and China. Since Deng Xiaoping re-opened China, many Western intellectuals, bearing the marks of cultural as well as political capital, carrying the skills and techniques of modern literary and cultural study, have found chances to travel, speak, and publish within both China and a Hong Kong newly redefined as a Special Administrative Region according to the One-Country/Two-Systems policy.

No self-aware American critic, no critic from anywhere at any time, can easily let pass the difficulties of such a situation of exchange and displacement. Wanting very much not to offer mere material or technique for appropriation and imitation by students and younger colleagues, I hoped rather to present a narrative of Western criticism that made the practices of that discipline transparently available as a regime of human life rather than as either a disciplinary formation or a business-like profession. In the figure of Stanley Fish and his lesser avatars, these two collapse into one.

As an American speaking guest, I hoped to make use of what I knew would be my audience's thorough knowledge of the English traditions. I wanted to align them with certain European-wide and American practices in part to denigrate the Englishness of colonial residue — as we find it, for example, in the practices of Practical Criticism — and the professionalism of newer jargons and alignments — including postcolonialism and multiculturalism. These last are, after all, very much residues of imperial power and practice and often their repetition. As I said frequently to my hosts, I hoped for the time when we might all speak of criticism with a common sense of its general qualities shaped by and aimed at the particular, regional, and international realities in which they sit.

To this end, it seemed best to test the case for historicism and its philological humanistic alliances with the primacy of poetry. Therefore, I begin with Vico and some of his sources and move through an unusual set of figures, some like Auerbach and Said clearly in his tradition, others like Mill and Foucault, who are not. I want to press the possibilities of rethinking the historicist humanists' discovery that history and not nature defines the species, that is, in the sense of Marx's great formula, that the human makes not only history but in the process makes itself as the historical species, as the species of history. This brought me to the position of arguing against what an audience member once called "pure literary criticism," by which she meant some echo of Practical Criticism that aimed at an ahistorical and apolitical demonstration of textual meaning and form. This residue of colonial British power aligns with a much more American form of emerging global mediocrity, that is, an historical and social disinterestedness that masks itself as professionalism. Positively, I show that criticism cannot be but as an engaged form of human will and action, learned in all the ways that philology once romanticized — or nearly so — and aware of its obligation to enable and support poesis as the general capacity of human cultural production as a means of and place for human completion of its own potential. In terms of war, which seems to come so easily to my tongue these days, criticism is both shield and spear, and those who would deny those uses are not critics.

Edward W. Said stands out as the great model for literary humanists in the struggle to reassert criticism's deepest and broadest political and cultural responsibilities. Those who know Said's work (and mine) will recognize the depth of his influence on these lectures, both in their commitment to historical humanism and a certain idea of the engaged critical intellectual. Moreover, such readers will recognize that I try to develop specific lines of thought that Said set in motion. For example, late in his career, Said elaborated a notion of culture as contrapuntal, which was his way of noting that culture does not yield to reductive analysis. He also argued that what he called "the politics of blame" had no monopoly on virtue. As strong a critic as he was of European colonialism and Orientalism, Said nonetheless appreciated and traced the complex contributions to human history, knowledge, and thinking that occurred within those reprehensible practices. Said would never have rested in a postcolonialist dismissal of the great nineteenth-century British intellectuals, condemning, for example, the Dickens of *Great Expectations* for its "unelaborated" treatment of Australia and its colonial relation to the U.K. Rather, Said took such texts for what work they did and might still do, opening them (and us) to historical awareness of their role in the creation as well as reflection of an imperial system that saturated British culture. Nevertheless, he did these things while at the same time recognizing and extending critically Dickens's contributions to the aesthetic modes of displaying the situation of the human and its potential. In a similar way, I engage here with John Stuart Mill, setting aside, for the moment, the postcolonial critical analysis of him as a colonialist, a chauvinist, and an implicit racist. I concede from the beginning the horrible truth of Mill's limitations not to dismiss, forgive, or forget them, but to explore other questions that a postcolonial indictment might disallow. For example, I use Mill to ask how essential classical liberalism is or was to the developments of historical humanism as they emerged from the European Renaissance. I do this, in part, because the advantages of liberal societies based on which the critique of liberalism is often launched are under attack both in the North Atlantic world and elsewhere in Asia and parts of the developing world. I insist that a form of appreciation of historical humanism obliges a serious look at liberal society's values and institutions if ever the dream to transcend their limits is to emerge in material forms.

I also follow Said in standing against the quietism of certain kinds of professionalism and "specialization." Said's objections to specialists' influence is commonplace at first sight — it preempts the desires and wisdom of all others and derives from self-legitimating institutions and discourses — but develops into an important element in his thinking about criticism and the civic role of the critic, which in retrospect approximates a classical, almost Ciceronian, view. I consider his passionate but witty and relentless criticism of Yasser Arafat and Samuel Huntington to be paradigms of how critics, motivated by love, a sense of responsibility for the species' future, and a loathing of injustice, should resist the arrogance of power and the ignominy of self-indulgence. Academic professionals who practice their own specialties merely within those self-legitimating systems and structures do not deserve the name "critic," except by circumstance. As Said argued about American-style deconstruction in the late 1970s, such practitioners become so absorbed in the importance of their own acts and judgments that they misplace their visions of themselves and things for views of the world. Famously, Said asked of deconstruction, what if a Martian came to earth, hearing all the talk of revolutionary overthrow of capital, phallogocentrism, metaphysics, and so on — what if that Martian looked around and asked, "What has changed? Has the state fallen? Has tyranny ended?"[1]

In contrast to Said's engaged critical humanism, Stanley Fish's free-market[2] professionalism has set the tone for many who came out of and after this period. I insist here that these matters concern not only U.S.-based academic professionals, but in part because of U.S. prominence and the power of certain discursive practices, academics spread throughout the world where certain modes of professional practice have standing. Arguing against Said's criticisms, Fish insists that even the critique of professionalism is a form of professionalism and so advocated a kind of careerist honesty, represented nicely by Fish's own simultaneous investment in law school teaching and academic administration and now the blogosphere. Reviewing the Said / Fish exchanges of the 1970s and their career paths and status, we find things of great interest. I contend, sadly, that Fish has won the debate by historical outcome.

Of course, Edward W. Said is a much more prominent intellectual internationally than Fish. Reviewing Google's data on searches makes that very clear.[3] My arguments rest on the perception that Fish is merely a figure around whom unfortunate elements in tradition and current practice in advanced academic work coalesce. I am concerned with issues and problems present in the Western critical tradition and, as the long readings of the Italian, Vico, and the Englishman, Mill indicate, the traditions I am surveying and judging have origins and consequences outside the United States. To suggest that my perspective is too much U.S.-focused is to neglect the comparative range of these lectures and to ignore the importance of U.S. practice in a world where, for better or worse, the United States and English, to say nothing of American universities, are dominant forces.

The other topic that might seem to some to be of mostly U.S. interest, that is, torture, is certainly not and only a most provincial reader would deny both the unfortunately large number of torturers there are in the world and the ill effects of the American Republic's unfortunate association with torture on the progress of political modernization. Furthermore, I intend to show that it matters profoundly that Western culture and criticism have developed in such a way as to suggest inseparability between the outcome of poetry as of a work of the human subject and of torture upon the body and so subjectivity, itself. Indeed, I claim that the forces that engage themselves in torture, that legitimate it, and that derive its effectiveness from science stand in diametric opposition to those that understand how human work in poetics produces an organized subjectivity that can itself allow the species to fulfill its capacities as historical, as self-made, and as guided by a desire for perfection.

I am not the first person to discuss the horrible effects of U.S. involvement in torture since the events of September 11. Nor am I the first to recognize that there are global implications to such horrors as Abu Ghraib and Guantanamo Bay. I am certainly not the first literary critic to attend to torture. I might be, however, the first to contend that poesis is the counterpoint to torture and that there are deep civilizational and species implications in the choice of power for torture over and against poesis as the unique human ability to make history according to humanity's best potential for subject creation. I hope to show that there are conflicts between historicist and analytic traditions of thinking in the modern Western world and that from the ahistorical, anti-literary tradition of analysis, it is much harder to muster opposition to torture or to see the horrors of torture as a special form of modernity's capacity for human self-destruction and, indeed, even eco-destruction. This last set of claims these pages present provocatively since lectures do not provide, or demand, the thorough demonstration associated with thesis-length examination of such large historical problems. Arendt's great book on totalitarianism stands out as a model for the examination of such topics and claims, but these lectures do not afford the chance for that kind of work.

Critics of American foreign and police policies, especially since the coming of the George W. Bush regime, have written thousands of pages attacking or defending the use of severe interrogation methods in poor areas of American cities and in the so-called "war on terror." These lectures do not take those policies or books as their immediate subject. Among all the materials that I know on recent applications of torture by the U.S. government and some of its often-unacknowledged allies in this enterprise, none see in it quite the same world historical point as I. In a most apposite irony, I contend that the application of terror and the development of legal, political, and indeed moral arguments in its defense, especially in its defense as a necessary bulwark to buttress Western civilization, demonstrate intensely the necessity to embrace and develop the modern projects of secular historical humanism. It is this last point that also leads me to warn scholars and students to withhold support from, to resist the allure of, analytically based critique as a norm for critical practice. I try to expose both the alliances among various practitioners of critical analysis, such as Bacon and Descartes, and the quite important negative consequences of withdrawing critical humanism from prominence, indeed, from dominance in culture, with effects that make the resistance to torture and all the barbarism it implies more difficult. Put simply, those scholars who embrace the tradition of philosophical analysis as the basis for professional academic "literary" study fail to advance the civilizing processes of historical humanism and stand less well-armed than need be in the face of the torture question. This last makes clear as possible the need to embrace the historical humanist project both as its own species task in "perfecting" culture and society and as the proper measure of torture's barbarism. Those who support torture should learn the species cost of their barbaric politics and thinking.

I hope that my readers will be as charitable as my audiences have been and not believe that because I have not spoken directly about certain topics or movements I am unaware of them or have not considered them. I am sure that some readers will descry what I have done here as either too Western — I remind them of the assigned topic — or as showing no sign of current global realities or awareness of academic debates. Of course, it is possible to make other choices in working through these materials and indeed one could choose entirely different sets of topics, authors, and texts. I offer these merely as a record of one attempt, at one place, in one time. I hope that they have some value for the future, as they seemed to have when overly polite audiences listened for what must have seemed at times like forever.

1
Vico and Philological Criticism

Those who occupy the heights of power yearn for the immense and
the infinite.
— Giambattista Vico, *On the Study Methods of Our Time*

Beginning in 1699, the Neapolitan thinker and critic, Giambattista Vico,
opened each academic year at the University of Naples with an "Inaugural
Oration" delivered on October 18, the Feast Day of St. Luke. As Professor of
Rhetoric, it was his job to introduce new university students to the nature, aims,
and traditions of education while at the same time elaborating his own ever-
deepening sense of its components, purposes, and ideals.

His speech of 1708 was special for several reasons and in many ways. It was
lengthier, more formal, and more elaborate because he aimed it not only at his
students but also directly to those in power. In 1707, as part of the Europe-wide
"War of Spanish Succession" (1701–14), Austria had driven Spain from control
of Naples — a mark of the Spanish Empire's decline — and the University's
administration had decided to dedicate the opening academic ceremonies of
1708 to the new imperial ruler. Vico delivered his lecture, *On the Study Methods
of Our Time*, before the Austrian Emperor's representative who embodied the
all too secular competition between Joseph I and the Vatican. The Austrian
Viceroy and Captain General of Naples was Vincenzo Cardinal Grimani, whom
Pope Clement XI considered excommunicating for representing the Habsburgs'
interests with too much enthusiasm.[1] Keeping this setting in mind steadies our
sense of Vico's political interests in this lecture that is so evidently concerned
with educational theory and human anthropology. Vico laid out for the city's
political as well as intellectual and academic elites a daring and expansive
prospect of the pedagogic and civil purposes of intellectual method within the
university and the city to which it belonged.[2]

Nearly three hundred years later, faced with the welcome opportunity to speak under the auspices of the Faculty of Arts to an audience including post-graduates whose auditing credits them with study in method, I start a series of lectures by invoking Vico's grand accomplishment. I do so not because we are older and wiser and more modern than he — that is, not to correct or admonish — but also not because we should or can only be his poor echo, merely an anxious shadow of his original greatness. I bring Vico before you to start this series of talks because he is an essential figure in supporting and elaborating the small cadre of loving intellectual workers who study criticism, poesis, and power hoping to make something permanent of humanity's historical potential. The cadre is small but impressive, including Plato, Machiavelli, Aristotle, and Bacon for Vico and, for us, as I will suggest in succeeding talks, Erich Auerbach, Edward Said, William Empson, and others.

Although Vico's great work is the final edition of *The New Science* (1744), an exceedingly original, inventive, and difficult expression of a lifetime's reflection on poetry, education, law, philosophy, and politics, I will speak mostly about the 1708 oration, *De nostri temporis studiorum ratione* (*On the Study Methods of Our Time*).[3] I have two reasons for this choice: first, Vico's lecture is an excellent model and second, it anticipates a great deal of what follows in his career. With some additions and qualifications, we can maintain faith with his accomplishments.

All critical humanists must study Vico so they might decide if they will embrace not all the details of his program but the basic historical and aesthetic principles of his method and thinking. My aim is to encourage you to take him very seriously as an interlocutor in our collective work on and with literatures and literary cultures. I will contend throughout these lectures that literary humanists, scholars, and critics devoted to the *litterae humaniores* should think of themselves in ways that are now rather uncommon, unfashionable, and institutionally difficult to imagine and maintain. If we literary humanists do not know Vico well, we diminish our capacities and contribute to a cultural amnesia the effect of which is nothing less than barbarism. Vico himself and the tradition of work he exemplifies offer moral, intellectual, and political resources that our societies need and that, for the most part, academic professionals and their extramural contemporaries do not provide.

"Crisis" is a very overworked word in recent literary and cultural studies and its pervasiveness in the media's accounts of political and social events wears it thin. Cheapened language supports the dominant powers of the status quo, shielding them from suitable discussion, undermining the commonplaces, the topics, that thriving polities possess. Literary history suggests this has always been the case, from Thucydides' description of linguistic decay during the plague years of *The Peloponnesian Wars* to Camus's echo of that trope in *La Peste*. Writing in 1929, Samuel Beckett gave us to understand that cheapened or as he put it when speaking of global English, "polite language," becomes available again with new force in its very putrefaction and, he adds, this is a perfectly Vichian insight.[4]

If the media and political speech have hollowed out this essential word, "crisis," which like so many other words we will discuss became common in English during the Renaissance, then not only academic careerist repetition but also more grievous Gnostic forms of intellection further its undermining. Historically, the very conditions and practice that damaged this word bring it back. The *Oxford English Dictionary* shows that usage confirms what Beckett understood, that "crisis" has now become a vacuous gesture of repetition that as a plain placeholder in people's speech more than ironically, viciously, creates the familiar: "now applied esp. to times of difficulty, insecurity, and suspense in politics or commerce." Merely historical consciousness notes this contextualized usage and proposes various analyses of its causes. Vichian historical humanism, however, not only contextualizes, conceptualizes, and "historicizes" — but it remembers and releases the results of human labor, the commonplaces, embedded in the material language we inherit and should preserve. What has died in the anti-human, historical reading can recover, aiming to preserve not only past human work as a resource and tradition, but the very idea of the species as historically human. Beckett, speaking of the Vichian elements in Joyce's renewal of language, puts it this way: "There is an endless verbal germination, maturation, putrefaction, the cyclic dynamism of the intermediate. This reduction of various expressive media to their primitive economic directness, and the fusion of these primal essences into an assimilated medium for the exteriorization of thought, is pure Vico, and Vico, applied to the problem of style."[5]

We will return to the question of style at several points in these lectures, especially when we approach Vico's heir, Erich Auerbach's reading of Dante. For now, we follow Beckett's Joycean and Vichian authority to recover "crisis" for our usage, not only about our moment, but for the entire set of threats that Vico's work helps us see confront not only humanistic historicism but criticism and so our cultural polities, themselves. From the putrefaction of media and academic abuse, we dare to call the need societies and academic humanists face "critical," to designate the present configuration of intellectual and political forces a life-threatening crux in the fate of the human and its productions. Just what this threat is we can only begin to say until we follow Vico through his analyses. It involves the alignment of anti-humanistic, indeed Gnostic intellectual ambitions, with now common political authoritarianism that increasingly relies upon not only capital investment in new forms of corporatism, but persistent transformations in the nature and function of knowledge, and especially their effects upon education.

I find myself using the term "Gnostic" in this Vichian context in a way similar to Slavoj Žižek in an interview, "On Divine Self-Limitation and Revolutionary Love," from 2004.[6] Žižek's remarks work as a criticism of the contemporary heir to Desartes, Alain Badiou, and I allude to them here precisely for that reason. In substance, Žižek and I agree on what we mean by Gnosticism but we part ways over its value. Žižek fits his own anti-humanism and anti-historicism into an anti-secularism that warns against conceiving of the Western God of Jewish and Christian monotheism anthropocentrically.

Žižek embraces a kind of weak Gnosticism that, setting aside for the moment his claim of its Jewish origins, repeatedly appears in habits of mind that typify modern philosophy and physical science. We will see the second of these points later when we touch on remarks by great physicists. The Gnostic habit of mind is, however, much more pervasive in the humanities than it should be, common even among those who have little idea of its persistence in their work. In the Vichian context, not only do ancient thinkers such as the Stoics and moderns like Descartes and his heirs fall within this practice, but so do the many intellectuals who have faith in various sorts of anti-historicist practices to liberate us from the fallen ruined time of political limits.

Žižek states the matter simply at first: "The basic message of religion, to put it in a nutshell, is that humanity cannot stand on its own." A good Baconian, Žižek expresses his admiration for what he calls "Jewish iconoclasm," which he insists is not antagonistic to Christianity. Indeed, iconoclastic destructions of anthropocentrism find their fulfillment, he contends, in Christianity. Žižek's thinking has about it, though, a strange residue of perhaps Kierkegaardian meditation. His iconoclasm morphs into a familiar Protestant Incarnationalism so habitual and assuring, one presumes, as to be at home now in the Vatican. "Images of God," he writes, are not proscribed "because God is *tout autre*, beyond, and every image betrays him, but because the space of the divine is not up there, it's here, in human interactions, and I think this is perhaps only brought to a conclusion in Christianity."

Žižek recognizes at least one danger on the surface of his position, Gnosticism. He insists his pose only approaches Gnosticism, a fact that interests me much less than his definition of the Gnostic and his rather extraordinary naïveté that denial does not reveal truth.

Here I may be approaching not so much Gnosticism as certain not a little bit heretical twists [*sic*], because I want to say not only that humanity only knows God through Christ but also that only through Christ does God know himself. We all know that this is a well-known gnostic, or not so much gnostic as a certain mystic tradition or heretical move, this idea that our knowledge of God is divine self-knowledge, and so on.

This is so pathetic that we can only laugh at it. Importantly, though, it tells us a great deal about the motivation of the anti-historicism, anti-humanism of our times and Vico's. This new wave of Gnostic or near-Gnostic ambitions, coming after a generation that took seriously the idea that there could be no poetry after Auschwitz, that ruin was inevitable, reflects nothing less than an inability to stand in the face of human self-knowledge stripped of the comforting error of divine infusion. Politics seems unable to redeem time, and so the Christ appears, ready at hand to those with certain kinds of partial memories, ready to comfort us once more. The great courage of Vico's work, as I hope to make clear, is that the human is always without the divine; that the Incarnation — whether or not cast as religion — is a diversion from the human responsibility for civilization and the ecosystem.

Having invoked Adorno, I must mention his remarkable essay on commitment to sharpen my own objection to Žižek and those like him. (I will, however, follow Vico and warn against intellectual models.) Adorno carefully distinguished the crudities of engagement — closely identified with Sartre and elements in Brecht — to make clear the critical indeed utopian possibilities of art that honors its own highest formal obligations. Although Adorno carefully discriminated between his position and the traditional French value of art for art's sake, readers sometimes confuse the two. Art for art is not the alternative to engagement; rather, form manifests those human capacities that negate by the evidence of their very existence both the truth of existing norms and their necessity. The same kind of claim might be made for Gnostic ambitions such as Žižek's or even Badiou's. One way in which Vico helps us is to elaborate Adorno's position to discriminate those acts of mind, apparently true to themselves as counter to what they take to be "the dominant," which nonetheless willfully destroy the historical project of a humanity self-responsible and self-made, free of illusion and coveting divine reflection. Within the modern, in other words, are fully "modernized" tendencies to reversion, to religion, to supposed origins more authentic than the historicist humanism Vico's studies traced and theorized.

Vico opened his lecture of 1708, standing before the assembly of church, empire, and university, with a clear critique of the profound similarities between

Baconian intellectual ambition and the tyrannical potential of modern politics — and of the professors who evaded their responsibility to examine this alignment while practicing, narcissistically, in their own domains. Vico stands forth as an avatar of the *litterae humaniores* who transforms his tradition into the highest form of modernity, conceiving the human as having come into being historically and as having its best chance to fulfill its limited historical possibilities only within the consciousness, knowledge, and patience of finitude's humility.

Vico's thinking is historicist in at least three ways. First, it knows itself as emerging from his profound and patient study of Western civilizations' various stages, formations, and transformations. Second, it knows itself as having come into being as a mark of humanity's modernity, its movement from spiritualism, mere naturalism, and superstition. It knows this movement was a struggle against persistent pre-modern formations as well as their persistence in modern practices, especially as arrogant aspirations to infinitude of power and theory. Third, and finally, it transforms this historical modernity into the active memory of a modern humanist thinker who never forgets the finite, malleable, and imperfect nature of the species that always only inhabits history as its own product — indeed, despite its worst dishonest and murderous phantasms, as its only possible habitation.

Vico's humanistic legacy demands that literary intellectuals celebrate and honor human historicism and humans as historical. Moreover, it vivifies the persistent threats to the achievement of the human as historical. It characterizes them for us as not only anti-historical and anti-humanist but also as anti-human, doing this, again moreover, within an altogether historical human account of all the errors that immaturely hope to find redemptive infinitude, certainty, or permanent authoritarian rule. In other words, the close alignment between certain interesting intellectual and institutional practices in the domains of knowledge and education appear in all too clear relations with tyrannical state power that not only has no respect for historical memory and qualification, but little if any respect, at least in potential, for the human itself.[7] We will see evidence for this conjunction later on when we address directly the realities of "psychological torture," a regime of knowledge and power that in essence is anti-human and anti-historicist in the most profound sense. As we will see, Vico finds the best approaches to human possibilities in poetry, in poesis as the very form of human being, that is, in making or creating. Torture emerges as precisely the antithesis of poesis (what I will sometimes call poesy), that is, as the destruction of the historical humanity of a person who falls within its grasp. Torture exists as this horrible possibility as the result of a particular but long-time looming alignment between modern intellectual ambition and state authority. It is in the horrendous context of putrefied civil life for the species that the word "crisis" recovers its force. It had never lost it for those such as Auerbach and Said,[8] who knew that Vico's historical studies presented far too many cases of such arrogant "human" aspirations and their dreadful consequences to relapse into either indifferent professionalism or Gnostic servitude to the anti-human. Following Vico, such intellectuals saw, measured, and understood the disadvantages for life in those rejected options and chose instead to work within the historical traditions that formed them and the human to elaborate poesy, the creative, laborious, finite life of culture and civility. A combination of arrogant intellectual error and authoritarian violence, especially as together they destroy the very possibility of finite humanity and its limited perfectibility, threatens both as fact and as possibility all that poesy represents.

Vico starts his lecture expressing admiration for Francis Bacon's "small but priceless treatise" (*De dignitate et de augmentis scientiarum*) for emphasizing the value of knowledge production in modernity and specifying the particular disciplines and practices we should add to our tradition to "enlarge our stock of knowledge" (*SM* 3–4). Bacon and Vico share the classical and liberal ideal of perfectibility, but Bacon dreams of achieving this by expanding the domain of knowledge, indeed, by producing knowledge as a necessary and sufficient domain for human aspiration and activity: "so that human wisdom may be brought to complete perfection" (*SM* 4). Vico does not share Bacon's vision of the modern for two reasons. First, its totalizing ambition is reductive in a way that leaves behind all that tradition and older forms of life might offer to imagine and fulfill the aspiration to and practices of human wisdom. Second, it is not only willfully amnesiac but also violently arrogant and uncomfortably close in kind and ambition to then new forms of imperial and authoritarian political ambition. Vico's language, always precise, rewards the sort of attention that literary readers properly learn from the study of poems — this is a point which Vico himself insists upon later in his lecture.

Vico's lecture is closely critical of several classical as well as modern lines of thought, so it is wrong to try to place him simply on one side or the other of the debate between ancients and moderns.[9] Nonetheless, he has densely specific profound objections to certain forms of (amnesiac) modernity, not least their ignorant repetition of classical errors, and his analysis of their disadvantages begins with his remarks on Bacon:

But, while he discovers a new cosmos of sciences, the great Chancellor proves to be rather a pioneer of a completely new universe than a prospector of this world of ours. His vast demands so exceed the utmost extent of man's effort that he seems to have indicated how we fall short of achieving an absolutely complete system of sciences rather than how we may remedy our cultural gaps. (*SM* 4)

[Sed dum *novum Scientiarium* retegit *Orbem*, novo magis, quam nostro Terrarum Orbe se dignum probat. Etenim eius vasta desideria adeo humanum industriam exuperant, ut potius quid nobis ad absolutissimam Sapientiam nesessario desit, quam quod suppleri posit, ostendisse videatur.[10]]

Gianturco translates "retegit" with "pioneer" as he renders "probat" as prospect. His excellent notes do not record that the trope, "retegit Orbem," opens up or discloses a new world, derives from the *Aeneid*, in a line spoken by Juno to Venus, in conflict over Dido's fate and the fate of empires. Specifically, Juno says, "Venatum Aeneas unaque miserrima Dido / in nemus ire parant, ubi primos crastinus ortus extulerit Titan, radiisque retexerit orbem."[11] ["When tomorrow's Titan / first shows his rays of light, reveals the world, / Aeneas and unhappy Dido plan to hunt together in the forest."[12]] The great Chancellor's ambitions are, indeed, Titanic, placed in the echo of disaster, figured in a classical trope, and marked with a worry about the human aspiration to divine clarity and imperial power. This last is the first soft sounding of Vico's objections to those moderns who substitute totalizing regimes of knowledge for a more complex, nuanced, and entangling poetics that forestalls these ambitions with historical and practical experience and values other than analytic power — specifically, value associated with memory, language, imagination, poetry, eloquence, and prudence.

Gianturco's translation renders perfectly Vico's sense of the dangers inherent in Baconian ambitions. Throughout this lecture, Vico weighs the advantages and disadvantages of classical and modern study methods, which requires him to specify terms of measurement by comparison between practice, idea, and context. Bacon's grand ambition, totalizing, as it seems, has disadvantages inherent in its own values. Gianturco's "rather than" [*quam quod*] indicates a divide in history and human effort, a choice (even if it seems impersonal) to abandon the effort to supplement our culture, which alludes back to "this world of ours" [*nostro Terrarum Orbe*]. Bacon's project has the advantage of defining its own impossibility, given the finitude of human capacities in producing a complete and defining knowledge system, but it has the disadvantage of obscuring what is humanly possible, namely achievement as supplement within human activity.[13] Human effort is inadequate to the Baconian ambition but not to the process of cultural supplementation. The human, quite clearly, has its place in the cultural and has the cultural as its place. Vico's quick gesture in producing this figure that ties the human to work as and in culture anticipates the sonority of his epistemological claim that humans can only know what they make — a claim upon which all historical humanism comes to rest.

Baconian ambition not only has the disadvantage of turning mind, labor, and love away from culture as the needed and appropriate sphere of human achievement — disproving with its ambition its own legitimacy — but it has definite, unavoidable, and dire consequences as a subversion of what the human has made. This is an important moment in Vico and an important moment for those who would learn to isolate those claims to modernity that are themselves destructive of its very possibility. Vico's profound and long-lasting disagreements with Descartes derive both from his fear of Descartes's blindness to the consequences of his advocacy for analytic practices as the modern and from the regressive nature of Cartesian ambitions that repeat past errors and would reverse the emergent achievements of the historically human. Of course, Vico understands the modern to be the historical result of human effort to produce the human as historical, to produce wisdom of the human's foundational modern achievement, achieving and knowing its own historicality. That Cartesians claim to be modern, especially in the battle with the ancients, is obvious. Vico, as we shall see, indicts their claim with the charge that they ignorantly reproduce earlier moments of thought and practice and that they share a genealogy with political authoritarianism and with pre-modern anti-historicist practices of the sort modern historical humanity constantly struggled to survive.

Gianturco gives us "retegit" as pioneer because of the philological complexities involved in Vico's original, which this English nicely carries. "Pioneer" is not only a military term — fitting to the Virgilian echoes — that suggests a going ahead, a scouting out, and so an uncovering or disclosing in the sense of being among the first to clear or investigate a space or "world." The English also gives us the military sense so right to this context, of a sapper, an underminer — a Baconian who destroys the fortifications to conquer and displace. To replace an old world with a new — this is the apparent if repetitive paradigm of modernity.[14] Vico's point is not nostalgic, but proleptic, a dire warning. Not only is the Baconian regime of knowledge not compensatory or fit to the human but it is quite precisely conjoined with the Machiavellian politics that conflicting empires enact. "Thus Bacon acted in the intellectual field like the potentates of mighty empires, who, having gained supremacy in human affairs, squander great wealth in attempts against the order of Nature herself, by paving the seas with stones, mastering mountains with sail, and other vain exploits forbidden by nature" (*SM* 4). Vichian criticism is profoundly ethical as well as political: profligacy joined with arrogance indicts this model of self-described modernity. It is not that Bacon is "against" nature, against the finitude of human nature that is his greatest crime, or that he turns the human away from the constructive projects of supplementation. The Baconian exhausts both the inherited resources of human achievement by denying them care and transformation by perverting their results into a project, the very possibility of which depends upon the processes of human historical emergence that it would destroy. Stupidly, the Baconian project is self-consuming as well as destructive of the species' achievements. Its sin or error is in not recognizing itself either through its similarities to its own predecessors or judging accurately its own consequences — its advantages and disadvantages. Because the imperium of knowledge knows nothing of losses but only gains, it abhors comparative historicism that does not reduce merely to the taxonomy of contemporary power. Above all, since it does not understand that the relevance of human achievements is to the civility and vitality of human life and history and not to the tyranny of knowledge, it fails the test comparison should adduce, namely, which cultural practices and ways of knowing form the best mode of life. Moreover, arresting history in its own auto-telos, it reverses the emergence of the historically human, so denies the species its greatest accomplishment, and closes the future, as such, as a possibility for imagination and continued self-making. This arrogant ambition is a reversion that threatens barbarism, a point Vico makes by associating it with imperial power's ambitions, and that I will make here by disclosing the figure it forms with torture.

Vico contrasts "retegit Orbem" with "probat," as Gianturco contrasts pioneer with prospect. (Later in the lecture, Vico claims he would admire these pioneers if their predictions held, which he feels they will not.) Giving "nostro Terrarum Orbe se dignum probat" as prospect discloses several themes that sound valuably in Vico's work. Prospect is not only to look forward but also to look into, as prospectors do for minerals. More to the point, prospect means to turn in a certain way, to have a face turned toward "a specified direction; outlook, aspect, exposure." (Looking ahead to Auerbach on Dante, we will see that prospect involves a looking down and into.) To prospect is not only a verb but also something like a gerund; it adds to action's force the weight of a substantive, of an established attitude or fixed position that creates the very horizon it explores. The *OED* puts it this way: "A place which affords an open and extensive view; a look-out." It examines what is and establishes the possibility of probing, makes it a permanent way of being alert and thinking, of doing intellectual work. We know the trope from poetry, from Milton's prospect moments in *Paradise Lost* to Walt Whitman's grandly entitled *Democratic Vistas*. To view, or in terms that echo recent criticism, to enframe or spatialize is inherently different from the pioneering ambitions that align themselves with the profligacy of imperial powers.[15] Vico makes a sharp contrast between pioneering the effort to displace the prospective by the substitution of a new world for ours, and the project he describes, of placing knowledge and state ambitions within a larger ethical and political set of judgments and practices more likely to sustain historical humanity's admittedly limited efforts to supplement its cultural needs. "No doubt," Vico concludes following these opening remarks on Bacon, "all that man is given to know is, like man himself, limited and imperfect" (*SM* 4). It is inhuman and unreasonable to have expectations that go against these prospects, so much so that they come into being as violent barbarisms and uncaring fantasies of the type common among those who plan to substitute their worlds for ours. Rather than the anticipatory work of prospect or prolepsis, Bacon and Descartes undermine and pioneer. The difference appears subtle, but in Vico's historical thinking, it is the difference between regression to barbarism and serving the species' ambition to have a historical future as the field of its imagination and will.

As you can see, I have read Vico's opening paragraphs as a staging of the very complex human historicality and desire that education, the principle topic of this lecture, must address. From this subtly contrived literary set piece, Vico elaborates his carefully historicized and balanced analysis of the advantages and disadvantages of different life regimes as a set of choices confronting humans and especially intellectuals within the developments of human capacities called modernity. Vico claims that "Every study method may be said to be made up of three things: instruments, complementary aids, and the aim envisaged" (*SM* 6), and while his point is that it is an error to confuse the most recently invented technique or aim with a human advantage, he makes good use of these categories to do comparative period analyses.

We can approach Vico's main argument from either of two foci: his antagonism toward Cartesianism or his own set of important human values. Since these two structure his lecture in tandem, we must talk about them together.

Vico begins with a simple but basic point that he addresses not only to those in power but also to students: scholars and researchers must accept that study has aims — it is and never can be purposeless. Students and scholars might deny knowledge of or care for their work's aims or the effects of the practices they acquire, but that does not deny their existence and consequence. "Aims" always exist; the problem is to bring them under some sort of conscious intent. Indeed, Vico's comments stand as a prolepsis against conformism, inertia, and willessness. Above all, they start out from the judgment that study and scholarly work are inseparable from the civil world of prudence and eloquence, of politics and culture, and put in perspective the continuing and now all too common defenses of ideological disinterest or detachment of the sort associated with Stanley Fish and his disciples.[16] Michel Foucault used to describe the great majority of work done in disciplines as anonymous. Not only was Foucault interested in the regularities of power systems beyond the categories of myths of individualized creativity, but he also analyzed the persistence of power in projects not begun but carried out by the fields themselves, especially by the Baconian regimes of knowledge/power. For Vico, not admitting to or knowing of the central and necessary part aims play in all research and study is willful ignorance, self-serving embrace of the status quo, and an irresponsible because fundamental betrayal of self-preparation as a humanistic intellectual, indeed, as a historical human being. Vico puts the issue in a quite modern metaphor: "As for the aim, it should circulate, like a blood-stream, through the entire body of the learning process. Consequently, just as the blood's pulsation may best be studied at the spot where the arterial beat is most perceptible, so the aim of our study methods shall be treated at the point where it assumes the greatest prominence" (*SM* 6). Not only does Vico's "should" remind us that there is dead study and research but it tells us how uninteresting that is. It is not the same as anonymous work because it has no heartbeat, which alone makes the work interesting for any educator or humanist who wants to compare its values and prospects.

If we are to instruct students as to the need for work to have aims and alert them to the fact that anonymous work has aims not their own, then we must find a way to work out what seems to be a contradiction. Students cannot know the aims of certain disciplines or regimes of life without study and yet at the heart of study lay those aims. How are students to know prior to or even in the course of study? This question Vico answers simply: "As for the aim envisaged, although its attainment is subsequent to the process of learning, it should never be lost sight of by the learner, neither at the beginning nor during the entire learning process" (*SM* 6). Keeping the aim in sight during the learning is a specific instance of how the student, properly trained, probes our world, prospects, if you will — Vico's word here is "*spectare*." All study has intention and purpose almost, as it were, independently of those who develop from apprentices to masters; proper education must, however, from the beginning (*principio*) and throughout both form a sense of purposes' necessity and of the specific purposes structurally enabled by a living course of work. Mastery involves control more than rote — hence, as we will see, Vico's later dissatisfaction with modern philosophy's reenactment of the Pythagorean relation between master and auditor. Teachers, however, play a fundamental role in preparing students, that is, teachers must alert the students to the purposes coursing through the methods and positions they profess. This in turn requires that the professors know and understand what they do, not merely in terms of the other two aspects of method, namely instrumentalities and bibliographies, but in terms of the aims that they themselves embody and, almost virally, transmit.

Later in his lecture, Vico compares ancient education under a master philosopher — Aristotle and Socrates are differing paradigms — with the chaoses of modern university education. Entire faculties teach within a Baconian regime of knowledge but often from completely incoherent and competitive points of view. Rather than celebrate the supposed pleasures of liberal pluralism, Vico worries the consequences of an intellectual incoherence that, we might say, makes choices of method and purpose seem to be merely life or taste choices among a range of authorized positions. In other words, Vico worries about what now seems so common in and among literary studies, choosing a "research paradigm," which is merely only a licensed way of speaking, among competing modes. The lifeblood, so to speak, of this model is the cacophony among competitors.[17]

It is a given that each method of learning and each form of knowledge emerges from the even more important historical decision to subordinate — in Bacon's dream — human life to a domain of knowledge production and power. By contrast, the critical, ethical, and political task of educated, eloquent, and prudent citizens must be to know and judge the prospects and alliances inherent in all methods of study. Educators must prepare students to turn in the direction contemporary forces project to anticipate their outcomes and must do so by comparing the contemporary with what humans have already done, so that citizens can judge proposed and hidden but likely outcomes.

When Vico puts his thumb on the arteries of the most powerful contemporary methods, he finds "analysis" and "critique" beating there. In a word, Vico shows that despite the great technical power that derive from these techniques, which are so deeply rooted in Descartes's works as their philosophical and methodological bases, they diminish human capacities to educate citizen intellectuals in the tasks needed to create vibrant societies. Let me assure you that my interest in this part of Vico's work is not merely antiquarian. His thinking has persistent value precisely because he reveals that the anti-humanistic and anti-historicist errors active in Descartes's methods repeat earlier projects, especially those of the Greek Stoics, and establish the continuing Gnostic ambitions of philosophers and "critics" working now.

Vico's worries about Descartes find their strongest expression in a few pages from his book of 1710, *On the Most Ancient Wisdom of the Italians*,[18] upon which he worked when writing his 1709 oration on study methods. Not surprisingly, he makes similar political and civil objections to Descartes's project as he does to Bacon's, linking them both to excesses of power: "Descartes has done what those who become tyrants have always wanted to do."[19] Vico believes Bacon's ambitions are imperial whereas Descartes's are tyrannical. Who can separate or rank these horrors now? Vico's indictment of Descartes was relentless and although he sometimes expressed admiration for Descartes's achievements in mathematics and study, he never expressed sympathy for or alliance with any aspect of the Cartesian techniques of analysis and critique.

Bacon's overweening ambition to substitute a regime of knowledge for the prudence of history at least taught the limits of human capacity — it came to the acknowledged truth of human finitude — and despite its critique of the tribes' idols, it did not roll about in the glories of ignorance or the hatred of reading. Descartes, by contrast, and despite his own formation — we might say, betraying his own formation — advocated, taught, a line of work that misled the young, found followers whose repetitions of the master Descartes did not dismiss, and figurally urged the burning of libraries and the relegation of languages to the domain of the serving classes. Edward Said's book, *Beginnings: Intention and Method*,[20] rests upon Vico's thinking at no point more than in Said's critique of "filiations," the genealogical model represented by the English novel of imperial culture and by the lines of authority and influence that create filial relations between masters and ephebes. Vico's assault on Descartes is not only a critique of the master's methods and consequences, but also the (unethical and perhaps immoral) modalities of authority that inhere in their practices and assumptions. These last explain Vico's willingness to hurl the charge of tyranny.

Like Descartes, tyrants

> came to power by proclaiming the cause of freedom. But once they
> are assured of power, they become worse tyrants than the original
> oppressors. In fact, Descartes has caused the reading of other
> philosophers to be neglected by claiming that, through the force of
> natural light, any man can know as much as others ever knew. Young
> simpletons readily fall under his spell because the long labor of much
> reading is tiresome, and it is a great pleasure to the mind to learn so
> much so quickly. (184)

Later, Vico will insist on the likeness between the proper forms of prudent
education and reading, which it turns out share qualities with the very processes
of poesy. In this essay, however, his concerns are more mundane: Descartes
authorized ignorance; his authority both indulges the rather beastly form of
mental pleasure that comes with confident license in one's own methods, and
it destroys not merely historical understanding but the essential prospect of
comparison. Cartesians care not to know by comparison and cannot since their
assumption of "natural light," properly trained, throws a basket not only over
all other work but also over the very possibility that others' works might throw
their own light!

Having aligned the Cartesian practice with tyranny and ignorance, Vico
had no hesitation in painting Descartes as a liar who deceived the young. Not
only were his ideas foods for simpletons,

> But Descartes himself, although he can dissimulate the fact with the
> greatest art in what he says, was versatile in every sort of philosophy;
> he was celebrated the world over as a mathematician, solitary in a very
> lonely life, and what matters most of all, he had a mind the likes of
> which not every century can produce. A man of such parts can follow
> his own judgment if he will, but others cannot. Let them read as much
> as Descartes read in Plato, Aristotle, Epicurus, Augustine, Bacon, and
> Galileo. Let them meditate as hard as Descartes did in those long
> retreats of his. Then the world will have philosophers of equal worth.
> But though there is a Descartes and a natural light, there will always
> be lesser men than he. Descartes will reign among them and gather the
> fruit of that plan of wicked politics, to destroy completely those men
> through whom one has reached the peak of power. And here I protest
> that . . . I have said all these things a bit too clearly and at some length.
> (184–85)

Descartes achieved authority by charismatically inducing his interlocutors to
become auditors, in the process drowning out the acoustical complexities of
tradition, libraries, and languages. Moreover, he aspired to authority as if that

were the highest virtue and did so not only by obscuring the past but also by narrowing the prospects of the future.

Vico makes these harsh charges because he cannot imagine a society in which it is worth living, in which people should live, or would want to live, unless that society values memory and imagination and the futures it builds out of them. He loathes intellectuals who would displace historical human ambiguities with the coups d'états of such tyrannical gestures as Descartes. We might say that of all Vico's thinking, what matters most to students and those affiliated with his work is the need for enduring humility over and against ambition, especially the ambition for self-originating authority or its political simulacrum. Descartes's complex artificial gestures erased all evidence of his own derivative self-creation, of the conditions for the possibility of his own being, and in so doing, committed multiple crimes, not least of which is to deny the possibility for others to do the continuing work of self and civil formation except along the lines authoritarian doctrines pioneer.

Vico and Descartes have fundamentally different understandings of the history and role of philosophy. Vico always historicizes philosophy and the philosopher whereas the Cartesian project is actively anti-historical and anti-historicist, substituting analytic and critical modalities for the active study of history. Vico thinks about, judges the relationship between different societies and their philosophers, and weighs the consequences to society of the philosophers' practices and self-conception. Given that Vico is not simply on the side of the ancients, he has a carefully differentiated history of the Greek and Roman forms of philosophical practice that specifies their advantages and disadvantages. Vico does the history of philosophy in a way that challenges "philosophy"'s arrogant assertion to be alone capable of judging itself. The comparative historical method constellates philosophical practices and ideals not only by reference to historical context but also by reference to function, aims, values, and effects. Vico does the history of philosophy from the prospect of its effects upon the social world and the sort of work it enables humans to do in perfecting their finite selves.

"Philosophers," Vico writes, "have had no function in the world except to make the nations among whom they flourished affluent, skillful, able, acute, and reflective, so that men became open-minded, quick, magnanimous, imaginative, and prudent in their active life."[21] It might surprise us that Vico introduces mathematics into our discussion. Of course, there is good historical reason for this, since he lived through one of the greatest flourishings of mathematics in Western history. Descartes contributed immensely to the period's work, along with Leibniz, Newton, and others who imagined what Leibniz called a *mathesis universalis*. In his historical studies, Vico noted that nations flourished when philosophers sharply separated themselves from such projects: "When the community of letters was first established, philosophers contented themselves with probabilities and left it to the mathematicians to treat truth. While this scheme, of which we have evidence, was maintained in the world, Greece laid all the foundations of the sciences and arts. Those most happy centuries fostered plenty of incomparable republics, enterprises, works, and great words and deeds."[22]

Philosophers' concern with probabilities had a corollary in their interest in "topics," the value of which Vico derives from Aristotle. Aristotle opens his book, *Topics*, with this goal:

> Our treatise proposes to find a line of inquiry whereby we shall be able to reason from opinions that are generally accepted about every problem propounded to us, and also shall ourselves, when standing up to an argument, avoid saying anything that will obstruct us. First, then, we must say what reasoning is, and what its varieties are, in order to grasp dialectical deduction: for this is the object of our search in the treatise before us. . . . Things are true and primitive which are convincing on the strength not of anything else but of themselves; for in regard to the first principles of science it is improper to ask any further for the why and wherefore of them; each of the first principles should command belief in and by itself. On the other hand, those opinions are reputable which are accepted by everyone or the majority or by the wise — i.e. by all, or by the majority, or by the most notable and reputable of them.[23]

Dialectical thinking does not aspire to the certainties of truth mathematics identified as "first principles." These are self-evident, unavailable for genetic inquiry. Mathematics had, according to Vico, "promoted in men a sense of order and developed a sense of beauty, fitness, and consistency." Stoicism, however, misapplied the rules and standards of mathematics to philosophy, sapping dialectical thinking by calling its results into question as socially constructed rather than epistemologically certain. The Stoics sloganeered their pioneering efforts into what Vico calls "their pompous maxim: 'The wise man has no mere opinions.'"[24] Vico reads the Stoics symptomatically as what we might call the first appearance of an impossible-to-eradicate virus that parasitically nourishes itself upon the "community of letters" by repeatedly emerging with a bag of powerful weapons that are dangerous threats. In this case, the Stoics' ambitions not only undermined the topical philosophies but also prepared the ground for their own subversion by the skeptics, a point that matters profoundly to Vico because to modern skeptics Cartesians have no response.

In his debates with Cartesians in Italy and elsewhere, Vico produced a historicized account of the consequences of differing philosophical authority and ambition. While the classical philosophers produced the best possible conditions for art, intelligence, beauty, and "incomparable republics," the Stoics epitomized an aggressive mentality that both reduced the complexities of reason to one dimension and cleared the way for even more destructive thought practices to follow.

If Aristotle had conceded the existence of several forms of reason and variously valuable outcomes to their implementation, the Stoics had grievously assaulted the traditional and social nature of the topics, of reason based on commonplaces that enjoyed consent, by specializing philosophy within the project of establishing and thinking from first principles. This proto *mathesis universalis* seemingly paradoxically displaced mathematics by co-opting its functions into general philosophy. As Vico puts it, "The school of the Stoics arose, and in its ambition, it aimed to disrupt the established order and to replace mathematics with their pompous maxim. . . . And the republic of the learned had nothing better to benefit by." The Stoic displacement of mathematics into philosophy destroyed dialectical reason and abrogated education in the topics, so that memory and imagination — learning and poesy — lost status and influence. Moreover, their intellectual ambition, by undermining the authority of the topics, created the ground of their own defeat by skeptics who offered critiques of Stoic truth claims that the latter could not defend. In the triple succession among dialectics / topics, Stoicism, and skepticism, Vico sees both cultural tragedy and the infection that persists in Cartesianism despite the human labor that created the consciousness and fact of human historicality. That last in the resumption of societies that sustain and depend upon a community of letters, a possibility that Descartes's assault on learning, as we will see, shows to be fragile, never assured.

If "the republic of the learned" had nothing better than Stoicism to benefit from, then its tragedy lay in the parricidal heirs Stoicism summoned into being: "a quite opposite order [of philosophers], the skeptics, arose who were completely useless to society. They found occasion for scandal in the Stoics, since they saw the latter were asserting doubtful propositions as true, so they set themselves to doubt everything. The republic of the learned was destroyed by the barbarians, and only after long centuries was it restored on the same basis, so that the domain of philosophers was the probable, whereas truth was the domain of the mathematicians."[25] We can easily read Vico as proleptic, as prefiguring Nietzsche and Foucault's analyses of the power of truth-discourse, but accurate as that belated reading might seem, it does some injustice to Vico's determination to indict intellectuals for the choice to indulge ambition barbarically by corrupting the proper attitude toward the truth.

Vico does not resolve "truth" into a domain of inescapable games of power or efficacy. Rather, he insists that "truth" has a dignity that the assaults, in truth's name, on the topical, the probabilities, and the dialectical have destroyed with horrendous consequences. Vico insists that societies flourish by properly venerating "truth" within thoughtful institutional structures and practices that, as in Aristotle's *Topics*, admit its multifaceted, multifunctional existence. There is "truth" in probability but philosophers, technicians, and politicians can and do instrumentalize "truth" as science, mathesis, or first principles to sap the authority of probability not to allow truth and freedom to flourish — no matter how often claimed — but to enable those games of tyranny that Vico recognizes in Bacon and Descartes. Moreover, that tyranny comes at the expense not only of particular memories and traditions, but also of the very possibility of their existence and function since mathesis replaces them with supposedly higher goals and imperium over-rules them by producing "new traditions."[26]

Vico did not believe that Descartes had successfully defended his position from skeptical criticism, and so Vico warned that modern historical humanity faced consequences similar to those visited by the barbarians in the ancient world. "Barbarians," in this case, refers neither to ethnically non-Greeks nor to those who ended the Roman Empire from the north. "Barbarian" refers to those pioneering intellectuals who visited "independence" and ignorance upon truth and the social world. Vico's short historical narrative makes clear his understanding and lays out the values underpinning the foundations of his 1708 oration. Above all, his extraordinary commitment to truth stands out.

Ancient and modern barbarians alike cheapened truth by applying in its name devices that were out of place. The Stoics made *sorites*[27] a symptom of their abuse as Cartesians did *demonstration*. As the first is an abuse of logic, the second, "extended to include probable reasoning and sometimes what is plainly false, has profaned the veneration for truth." Vico continually indicts his interlocutors for not weighing the outcomes, the advantages and disadvantages, resulting from "innovation." In itself, this failure of judgment characterizes the imperial ambitions of the pioneering class. More important, it brings into sharp focus the nature of intellectual arrogance and its human cost: "Now we can see the advances, but we do not reckon the great loss that accrues to it, not to speak of the much greater loss that will shortly accrue because our own good sense has been made the regulator of truth." If the instrumentalization of truth, the habitual frequency of its invocation in the testing of every merely probable — only to show, of course, that it *is* merely without epistemological or mathematical foundation — destroys truth's dignity by making it the engine in an all-too-familiar gambit of de-authorization, that immediate loss prepares for worse. What is that "worse," for Vico? Nothing less than the loss of those skills essential to renewing the republic of the learned, which will leave each of our generations dependent only upon itself:

> Now we can see the advances, but we do not reckon the great loss that accrues to it, not to speak of the much greater loss that will shortly accrue because our own good sense has been made the regulator of the truth. For now, the ancient philosophers are not read, or very seldom read. This will be costly because the mind is like a soil that though it may be fertile with mother wit, becomes barren in a short time if it is not fertilized with varied reading. And if it at times an ancient philosopher is read, he is read in translation, because today, on the authority of Descartes, the study of languages is considered useless. For Descartes used to say, "To know Latin is to know no more than Cicero's servant girl."[28]

Of course, those "in power" have good reason to obstruct the comparative knowledge, the historical knowledge, that might make dominant assumptions and practices seem to be arbitrary. Therefore, Cartesianism appears as an early version of the official discourse an emerging dominant always requires to assure its own position. The consequences of such self-interest, though, are relatively minor compared with the effect of such amnesia on the species itself. The structural consequences are much worse, threatening a reversion to barbarism.

All the human effort that went into the elaboration of the species as historical humanity disappears in this forgetting. The loss of languages is metonymically the loss of memory, of knowledge, of interest in the deposited processes of human transformation, and the impossibility of prospecting in the shared labor of human culture. Language is the enduring depository of achievement, of possibility, and, most important, of human reconciliation to its own finitude. The politics of such reconciliation is the opposite of imperium and its Baconian or Cartesian modes of intellectual arrogance.

2
Philology and Poetry, The Case against Descartes

I took us through some very strong moments in Vico's work to prepare us to see the demands his thinking makes on us at times like ours when it is very easy to inherit the influence of his great opponents such as Descartes. More important, though, the main obstacle to an appreciation of Vico as a predecessor today is, in fact, the principle reason why we must make the effort. Many major strands in current politics are authoritarian and imperial,[1] precisely the threats Vico's writings resist, making them more valuable in defense of liberty than at any time in recent history. What I mean is rather simple if dreadful. I take the United States as an example in this discussion not only because I am most qualified to discuss it but because reasonable people can agree that America's power and internal politics now make it a central (if troubling) player in world history. The rise of China (and perhaps India), the continuing processes of global financialization, and the European Union's desire to act as a player almost entirely in the field of what political scientists call "soft power" — all these taken together create crises for the United States and opportunities that especially neo-conservative and religious thinkers have exploited under the sign of terror to enhance authoritarianism of a kind that too many intellectuals in the humanities take as evidence of the end of politics[2] and the human.[3] It is vitally important that historical humanism have defenders who support the important body of critical work now done in institutions that are under pressure from this authoritarian politics. They must argue strongly in defense of that humanism against not only the egregious public phenomena that threaten its independent survival but also against those mistaken or erroneous intellectual efforts that, having their parallels in Stoicism and Cartesianism, lead intellectuals into practices that support authoritarian imperialism or seduce them into dangerous irrelevance. In the first lecture, I chose simply to call these last groups by the term, "Gnostic."

In this lecture, I intend to make a more modest and perhaps temperate two-part argument. I want to present more of Vico's reasons for distrusting the Cartesian processes especially as they establish themselves as institutional norms. (I hasten to add that I am aware that there were numerous thinkers after Descartes who depend upon his ingenuity while providing alternatives to some of his conclusions. None that I know seems now to offer as valuable an alternative as Vico does.) I also want to outline more of the positive achievements a Vichian poetics offers our critical intellectual projects and so our lives as citizens who hope to live within the most liberal forms of just and free societies. In other words, a strong Vichian criticism of that compounded figure "Bacon" / "Descartes" — that is, the arrogant intellectual who carries out what politicians can often only dare — emerges from and is part of the desire to produce citizens who know the wish for better societies and accept the obligations of working for them. Vichians do not work merely by negative critique — despite its value — but toward the extensive production of those goods needed to supplement the societies we have as they aspire to their own perfected liberties.

In particular, I hope to convince you that Vico is remarkable for showing us that the best parts of human life consist in creating the human itself as a being self-conscious of itself as its own best historical creation or creature. I hope also to show that for Vico this process is what we might properly call an aspiration for perfection. This aspiration takes the form of exactly that which Bacon's work obstructs, namely, the need to elaborate and supplement our culture's achievements so that our efforts are not lost, liberty remains a virtue worth struggling for, and human works enhance the conditions for the species' capacities to develop a respect for the virtues of its own efforts. I especially want to prepare the grounds for an historical and critical argument by stressing Vico's insights into the difficult necessity of accomplishing the strengths of modern humanity as complexly balanced, able to deal with its own temptations and vulnerabilities, able to recognize and resist the political and intellectual allure of promised universalism, evolutionary stasis, and authoritarian security. Vico has only recently reemerged[4] as one of the West's greatest thinkers about poetry and poesis. I hope to generalize from his poetics a theory of human historical self-making that at its most daring gets carried out under the term, perfection — a term that we all know contains the most profound dangers, often in the form of alluring enchantments.

Vico's poetics rests upon a strong ethic that discloses the possibility of balanced imaginative existence of a kind that is the true goal of perfectionist ambition and that, as such, avoids the dangers inhering in what, in the Vichian system, is the arrogant perfectionism of tyrannous desires. This last set of insights I will sloganeer as "torture is the diametrical opposite of poetry," a slogan that will bring us from Vico through Mill, the most useful of perfectionist liberals, to the more radical figure of Foucault, before ending in the still somewhat underestimated critic, William Empson.

The intellectual center of *On the Study Methods of Our Time* is the contrast between philosophical analysis and poetics. These lectures assume that too much of recent criticism has enjoyed a romance with philosophy, drawing upon derivatives of early modern philosophy for means to discuss literature, culture, and intellectual practice. Giving a good historical account of this event would require time and detail that would draw us away from our own purposes. Fortunately, Vico's lecture stages the conflict between analytic philosophy and poetics proleptically, anticipating the consequences of choosing to develop intellectual life along one modern path rather than another.

Ever since Wordsworth, of course, a simple cry has resonated among some poets, critics, and ordinary readers: "We murder to dissect."[5] Neither Vico nor I wish to defend this too often sentimental and anti-intellectual gesture of affective ideology or common sense. Cartesian analysis does indeed murder in Vico's eyes, but it murders not feeling or immediate perception of nature but the wide-ranging potential of human intellect and effort. Most especially, it murders history and creation.

Because of his deep interest in the proper way to form young minds, Vico counterpoises education in topics to education in analytic techniques. What is the issue? For Vico, it is deceptively simple: Historical human life is not and cannot be lived along lines assumed by the forms of analytic demonstration. Hence, his objection to analysis as a mode and to demonstration extended into areas where, as a form of intellectual work, it is a misfit, does the wrong things, and cannot but produce undesirable results. One basis for Vico's discussion is, as I suggested last time, Aristotle's *Topics*, which provides an account of various forms of reasoning and the different values, the differing contexts, in which each belongs. Learning to reason with topics better prepares citizens for political and artistic life precisely because it rests upon and reflects a proper understanding of the fact that humanity has developed to the point of being historical. This last fact means that social life and culture are always and everywhere the consequence of human work at self-formation, a task that cannot proceed on the restricted basis of analytic demonstration. Why not? Because such demonstration is both inherently ahistorical and so incapable of thinking its own historical implications among forms of politics and life that might well find in it, indeed, do find in its aspirations, assuring congruencies that the world of thought will support the politics of tyranny and empire.

Aristotle taught Vico that by forming a young mind in topics educators would create the conditions for advancing social worlds along the unavoidable lines of political struggle and artistic elaboration. Aristotle made basic distinctions between demonstrative reasoning, dialectical reasoning, and what he called contentious reasoning — all of which rest upon the differing status of premises as points of departure for the mind. In demonstration, the premises are "primary and true"; in dialectical reasoning, they are "generally accepted"; whereas contentious reasoning, "starts from opinions that seem to be reputable, but are not really such."[6] Vico insists that education must form minds by training in the topics because young minds developmentally evince powerful memories and imaginations, and are well-suited to the proper task of remembering and inventing arguments precisely to test their certainty and utility. The analytic method, by contrast, has only two general movements: learn the modalities of demonstration and discredit the seeming truth claims of those arguments that do not meet demonstration's standards. As we have already seen, Vico tells us that this ploy replicates the Stoics' bid for authority and devastates the society that rests upon it, vulnerable as its ideas and standards become to skepticism. As if this were not enough of an objection, Vico adds that education in analytic demonstration, when it comes at the expense of education in *ars topica* disguises or misrepresents the very nature of human and natural life, attempting to substitute arrogated mathematical necessity for the fact of and skills needed in a world of incertitude.

I want to emphasize an important conclusion that derives from Vico's work in these areas, namely that literary criticism does not and cannot coexist with the practices of analytic demonstration. This seems absurd, of course, since "critique" is the self-defining practical standard of the greatest European philosophers and their traditions, which have much influenced literature and literary studies. Literary critics have to clarify terms. Vico himself assigns the term, "criticism," to the practices of Cartesian analytics and declares it "the art of true speech" (*SM* 15). "Truth" here abides in the analysts' love for necessary demonstration. *Ars topica* over and against analysis is the art of "eloquence" as topics are "the art of finding 'the medium'" (*SM* 15). Vico uses this medieval term in a thoroughly modern way. The medium is scholastically the "middle term" but more important in this context, it also refers to the means of presentation, especially of an argument's most persuasive terms. When educators form a young mind in the topics those minds learn how to find the most effective "*loci*" or "lines of argument" that allow citizens, artists, or politicians "to grasp extemporaneously the elements of persuasion inherent in any question or case" (*SM* 15).

If critique resides in "the art of true speech," then criticism — as poetic and political life require it — must reside in the spontaneous inferential comprehension that eloquence requires and the mind needs to achieve certainty among opinions. Vico helps us make a broad and crucial distinction between critique and criticism. Critique belongs to the tradition of Stoicism, analytics, and the romance of truth — a tradition vulnerable to the specter of skepticism, its own daring claim for authority called into being as its best enemy. Criticism, thoroughly historical in its foundational awareness of uncertainty in human life and in nature, is not tempted by truth's revelations and seeming power. Friedrich Nietzsche made a lengthy tale of truth's romantic possibilities, of philosophers' clumsy efforts at winning the object of their desire; but, more to the point, the intellect, "unseduced" we might say, knows itself capable of other things than this attachment to the fantasy object of its self-allure.[7] The parallel between this intellectual or "philosophical" ambition to obtain the beloved that assures the lover's authority and the politics that would secure its own domination is not mere analogy. We could call what these mental and political processes lack abnegation, except that humility and endurance are better, more positive names, for the virtues civilization requires from intelligence.

What is lacking in analysis and so in critique? The answer is simpler than the productive results of analytic method make it seem. Analytic critique makes best use of the substantive comparative material advantages modernity provides students and teachers over the study methods of the ancients. Such inventions as libraries, printing presses, universities as "institutions of learning" — these all illustrate modernity's "reduction to systematic rules, of a number of subjects which the Ancients were wont to entrust to practical common sense" (*SM* 8). Critical analysis systematizes and theoretically underpins all these institutional material developments with an analogously reductive program that reciprocally legitimates those institutions upon which its own efficacy depends. Moreover, these modern reductions exist, as Vico's comments on Bacon suggest, in an exact relation to the emerging state system's tendencies to authoritarian and imperial centralization and reduction. Vico puts the matter lucidly: "As for the aim of all kinds of intellectual pursuits: one only is kept in view, one is pursued, one is honored by all: Truth" (*SM* 9). If Vico's early mention of Bacon made it seem as if the systematizing of encyclopedic knowledge were the modern intellectual ambition parallel to state ambitions, then his commentary on analytic critique opens a supplementary line of thought, one that draws an important implied relation between "Truth" and sovereignty and opens the relation to questioning of a kind that compels Baconian and Cartesian alike to confront the political consequences of their desires and alliances.[8] Lest these consequences seem only abstract, let me give a brief example of how material they can be.

English Common Law and perhaps even the Magna Carta prohibited torture, which was not a long-standing part of English tradition, but when he was Chancellor, Lord Bacon advocated torture as an inherent sovereign power.[9] In 1619, Bacon recommended torture to King James in a possible case of treason: "If it may not be done otherwise, it is fit Peacock be put to torture. He deserveth it as well as Peacham did."[10] As we shall see, the modern compulsion to a regime of truth that displaces the historical world of certainty and uncertainty has much to do with the destruction of the human subject and liberal institutional controls upon power that take place in torture and its regimes.

Vico patiently reconstructs Cartesianism's view of its own accomplishment, chief among which is a victory over the classical period's legacy of doubt. "Modern philosophical critique," Vico writes of Cartesians' presumption, "supplies us with a fundamental verity of which we can be certain even when assailed by doubt. That critique could rout the skepticism even of the New Academy" (*SM* 9). We have already seen Vico's disproof of this claim in his remarks from 1711 and 1712, rebutting objections to his book, *On the Most Ancient Wisdom of the Italians*. What matters to us now is developing Vico's sense of what critique leaves out so we might have a more human and less politically dangerous intellectual practice that deserves the name "criticism."[11]

First, we must repeat Vico's illustration that analytic critique polemically stands against historical knowledge, especially against the sort of philological knowledge of culture and politics achieved by a study of languages and literatures — the domain of criticism. In opposition to Descartes, Vico demonstrates that for ancients and moderns alike, language and literature are essential to educate thinking minds of citizens. "Complementary aids," Vico writes, "are also works of literature and of the fine arts whose excellence designates them as patterns of perfection." This last term recurs increasingly not only in Vico but liberal and radical thinkers after him. It is a term central to educational and cultural thinking that grounds increasingly the practices, even ironic practices, of the best literary criticism. (I hope we will see this not only in Mill but also in Empson.)

Second, analytic critique extends its technique and desire from a domain where it claims to demonstrate its universal applicability — mathematics and physics — to domains of human life where its fitness depends upon suspending the historical uncertainties and human agencies of political intellectual culture. (It is at this hinge or liaison that we find the destruction of the subject congruent with the destruction of democracy, of republics.) While Vico concedes that analysis has led to great accomplishments especially in geometry and physics, he nonetheless criticizes the implications and costs of the intellectual tendencies beneath them. Setting aside for the moment the question of geometry, to which Vico returns in the context of memory, he takes up analytic achievements in physics. His method is familiar. He describes his opponents' achieved view as accurately as possible:

> Modern scientists, seeking for guidance in their exploration of the dark pathways of nature, have introduced the geometrical [analytic] method into physics. Holding to this method as to Ariadne's thread, they can reach the end of their appointed journey. Do not consider them as groping practitioners of physics: they are to be viewed, instead, as the grand architects of this limitless fabric of the world: able to give a detailed account of the ensemble of principles according to which God has built this admirable structure of the cosmos. (*SM* 9–10)

We can see what bothers Vico about critique's ambitions — its universalism, its fascination with certainty — all of which he catches in the idea that physicists can "account" for God's plan. It would seem that as modern physics advanced analytically along Ariadne's thread, it became even more ambitious in its desire to achieve certainty of knowledge by coming near to God. Einstein used to say, "I want to know God's thoughts — the rest are mere details."[12] More to our point, Stephen Hawking has a Dedalian solution to the labyrinthine problem Ariadne solved: "if we discover a complete theory, it should in time be understandable by everyone, not just by a few scientists. Then we shall all, philosophers, scientists and just ordinary people, be able to take part in the discussion of the question of why it is that we and the universe exist. If we find the answer to that, it would be the ultimate triumph of human reason — for then we should know the mind of God."[13] For our purposes, the sort of arguments that philosophers of science might raise regarding needed discriminations among the mathematical methods of the Cartesians, Einstein, Hawking, and others — to say nothing of quantum and string theorists — matter very little. Vico's objections are important to those who wish to reassert the centrality of human historicism to the work of our knowledge producing culture and politics. As analytic critique unduly extends itself into the domains of human life to rule out as unimportant language and literature, so it misleads itself and others by conjuring the illusion that its proofs regarding nature provide certain knowledge, the truth of nature certified by its almighty status as the mirror of God's mind. Analytic physics creates semblances of truth only, masking both the uncertainty of nature and the weakness of its own method. If analytic geometry holds in its own domain it is because the human mind creates the propositions upon which its demonstrations rest.

This is not true of nature on analysts' own grounds: the mind of god humans can only know uncertainly. Were it otherwise, we would not only know through a mirror laws elsewhere reflected in our own reason, but "we would be capable of creating them *ex nihilo* as well" (*SM* 23). Having set aside all historicist knowledge and self-knowledge, analysts doing critique cannot have a perspective on their own efforts since, even as philosophers, they do "history" only from within their own regime or discourse. Criticism, however, since it takes the uncertainties of human history as the material of thought can see the extent and consequences, the placement of these analytical critiques. While they allow physics to achieve what seems to be, because this is what is desired, "apodeictic form" that practitioners can teach in "a plain, unadorned way," they also cost physics all eloquence and their forms all "aesthetic charm" (*SM* 24). Wherein lays the value of eloquence in physics? Vico's multilayered answer begins, as does so much else, with an emphasis upon the social, intellectual, cultural, and political outcomes of education. Analytic method is reductive and severe, "as severe as it is limited." I want to stress that Vico's objection is not an epistemological objection to reduction; rather it objects to the educational model that reduction implies. Moreover, his objection matters even now when professionalization within corporate universities moves education in the same direction. Ironically, Vico finds that analytic critique "is apt to smother the student's specifically philosophical faculty."

Vico's sense of philosophy is quite specifically poetic both in its echoes of the ancients and its anticipation of certain modernist critics. Analytic critique destroys the capacity for metaphor, a fact that Vico must discuss on the terrain of physics education since the Cartesian model, in advance, has ruled that the terrains of literature and language, history and politics, have no value in their truth games. In the gesture of condemning the Cartesians for their anti-philosophical results, Vico renews the place of literature. How does analytic critique educate? In the value of the increment and at the expense of the brilliant perception that forms the basis of eloquence. Vico concedes to the Cartesian that "quest" is the proper form of intellectual work, but apodeisis is neither the way nor the grail. "Our theory of physics," Vico remarks, "(in the process of learning as well as when mastered) moves forward by a constant and gradual series of small, closely concatenated steps." This Baconian ambition is a damaging educational practice and an amputated mental de-formation. It destroys the mind's "capacity to perceive the analogies existing between matters lying far apart and, apparently, most dissimilar." This is, of course, a remark that both criticizes Vico's opponents and names elements of his own practice as an ideal. Vico's mind is critical in perceiving despite distance — or, to put it negatively, Vico's mind and method resist the dogmatic constraints of experts, disciplinary bounds, and querulous trivializers who might ask such questions as, "what does Vichian thinking about Descartes have to do with the problem of torture in a society." Eloquence lies in the unbound mental capacity to perceive similarity where it may not appear. "It is this capacity which constitutes the source and principle of all ingenious, acute, and brilliant forms of expression" (*SM* 24).

In a word, this is metaphor, both the capacity to create the figure and the figure itself. To metaphorize is an essential capacity, one that educators must attempt to develop. It is not only an ability to express, but also a means of knowing, a capacity and record of perception, and importantly, a mode of critical invention, of poesis, that resists and supersedes the evidently known. To metaphorize is neither to produce encyclopedic knowledge à la Bacon nor to analyze and reduce à la Descartes. When Vico develops his objections to Cartesian physics by contrasting it with Euclidean geometry he reverses Plato's *Meno* to insist that teaching geometry activates and enhances the mind's ability to visualize and to link. Geometric perception aligns with metaphor in the way that Vico brings the language of geometry itself into play in describing metaphor's poetic function of disclosing patterns, alignments, and relations that otherwise remain unseen and undervalued. Not only does Vico link metaphor, eloquence, and geometry as valued means and goals of all productive education but also he helps us understand that they are themselves essential to the dual goals of human civilization: creative perception and critical freedom.

Critics can learn from Vico's objections to Cartesian method, from both his cautions and the values that underlie them. First, "geometrical method constitutes a hindrance in the way of an eloquent exposition of the principles of physics" — a careful reminder that achievement comes at a cost. As Edward Said would have put it, each increase in authority or capacity molests the will in its very ability to create or think.[14] Second, the hindrance analysis poses to eloquence is not habit of language use but incapacity of mind, a blunting of that "capacity to perceive analogies." Third, in its relentless pursuit of only one goal — apodeictic forms of expression and knowledge — analysis confuses "acuity of ideas" with acute brilliant expression, which depends upon the ability to metaphorize. Acute ideas Vico represents as a straight line: "tenuous, delicately refined." Ordinary innovation takes this form and education to this end is merely the formation of skill. Acute expression or eloquence requires two lines as representation. This is because, of course, the properly formed mind can see analogies across great distances and between things that seem deeply dissimilar. The one-dimensional, unidirectional acuity of ideas — the will to reductive apodeisis — neither crosses these distances nor perceives the appropriate similarities. Eloquence, we might say, exists at and because of the catachreses that occur when lines cross forming acute expressions that show the cost analytic reduction pays in allowing the mind and will to move only along the well-established line of inertia.

Over and against the reductive desire for apodeisis, Vico poses the complex richness of contingent human creation and human perception of history and nature. Over and against the self-imposed restrictions of the human will's capacity to invent, perceive, and express that resides in that desire, Vico posits metaphor, or if you will, poetry as the better mark of human capacity and the better master and measure of human education. Of metaphor Vico speaks only in superlatives, precisely because it is so perfect a form of human contingency: "Metaphor, the greatest and brightest ornament of forceful, distinguished speech, undoubtedly plays the first role in acute, figurative expression" (*SM* 24).

Vico is both Horatian and Ciceronian in what he has to say about eloquence: it provides pleasure and it moves the unformed to proper action and attitudes. "It is to the modes of thinking of an ignorant multitude that eloquence is particularly suited. . . . The pleasure imparted by an excellent speaker pleases everybody without exception" (*SM* 24–25). I want to stress that in our educational systems we too often forget the value of moving people and giving pleasure. Of course, demagogues do not forget and often succeed by satisfying the need for security that they first arouse by historically suitable appeals to fear. Indeed, recent politics remind us that demagogues prefer the lie, prefer power to the truth. While defending truth in the face of demagoguery is a crucial task for mature societies and educators, fetishizing truth as apodeisis or as part of an imperial regime of sovereign knowledge can be both politically ineffective and, indeed, in part culpable for creating intellectual standards not adequate to the political formation of minds and institutions. In this sense, the Baconian imperialist is not only complicit but also negligent. By contrast, the creature Vico calls "the skillful orator" operates within the domain of topics and "omits things that are well known" to move the auditors' minds to complete the line of thought: "his listeners are made to feel they are completing it themselves" (*SM* 25).

Cartesian analysis is not likely to produce intellectuals capable of political leadership — this we can concede. More important, though, the Cartesian project undervalues education as political formation and overvalues its own imperial alignments as a device to guide power. Put brutally, Cartesian education is no proper education for life in modern political societies except insofar as it is an accomplice of sovereign power that finds in apodeisis a parallel desire, an analog to its ambitions to arrange the world for the last time within its own imperium. If analysis has political fitness, it is for tyranny.

This harsh judgment stands against the admitted abuse of rhetoric and eloquence that since the ancient world thinkers have worried as a means of demagogy that might produce, in the modern world, the well-regulated tyranny of the majority. Modern scientific political advertising has its place in this history, but not as a form of eloquence and indeed for that very reason begs the question if eloquence can serve demagogy. In the Vichian spirit, the answer to this is no.

If as I tried to suggest in my first lecture, we must take seriously Vico's decision to present his early objections to Bacon and Descartes in political language that allies them each differently with abuses of power, then we must also take seriously the alternative mode of human formation that falls within the ideals of eloquence and metaphor. To do so requires that we see the politics of eloquence as inherently opposed to tyranny and the creative perception of metaphor as inherently opposed to tyranny's desire to arrest history in its own imperial dreams.

Nevertheless, we must face up to the prejudice that associates eloquence as much with political danger, the threat of popular manipulation, as with moral political, forensic, and critical good. The twentieth century provides ample evidence that this prejudice rests on solid grounds. Not only does popular culture reflect the association between eloquence of a sort and corruption, but also high critique does the same. In 1927, for example, the muckraking Nobel Prize–winning American novelist Sinclair Lewis published *Elmer Gantry,* a novel that closely follows the entangled relations between evangelistic religion and its enthusiastic rhetoric and the moral good. In 1960, the important American director, Richard Brooks, filmed *Elmer Gantry* with Burt Lancaster in the title role.[15] Brooks's film is contemporary not only with the developing force of post-war U.S. conservatism's reliance upon Christianity, but also with a strong intellectual development of Max Weber's thinking about charisma to account, in part, for political developments in Europe, America, and Asia during the early twentieth century. This last trend, to which belongs such countervailing work as Hannah Arendt's *Eichmann in Jerusalem* with its account of evil's banality, belonged to larger efforts to understand the subservience of populations to totalitarian rule. In effect, nothing less than the relation between democracy and human reason mattered to those worried about the industrial, institutional, and psychological effects — especially in the media — of charismatic eloquence and commanding appearance upon citizen subjects. For good reason, therefore, suspicions of eloquence became common among defenders of freedom, democracy, and the integrity of the human subject and its histories.[16]

Nonetheless, the histories of rhetoric, of literature, and of criticism often represent eloquence as the very basis of republican and democratic possibility, as a goal of education, as an essential means to human perfection, and as means as well as goal for thoughtful creativity. "Longinus," for example, notoriously praises the sublime as a form of style and capacity of human inspiration precisely for its abilities to move audiences far beyond their normal ranges of experience and feelings. Indeed, Longinus concludes his treatise with a complex allegory of the relations among sublimity, eloquence, and freedom. Longinus worries about the anomie of a social order that pursues wealth and riches above all else. He sounds like a reactionary defender of old times, but his modernity is thoroughly in keeping, as we shall see, with Mill's condemnation of the market in England and with Arendt's perception of the banality of evil and its reverse. "Summing up," Longinus concludes, "I maintained that among the banes of the natures which our age produces must be reckoned that half-heartedness in which the life of all of us with few exceptions is passed, for we do not labor or exert ourselves except for the sake of praise and pleasure, never for those solid benefits which are a worthy object of our own efforts and the respect of others."[17]

Longinus, we might say, embodies a risk that European Enlightenment thinkers would not willingly accept, preferring the control of reasoned ethics to an aspiring poetics that clearly invokes not only the importance of transport but also its power: "The effect of elevated language upon an audience is not persuasion but transport.[18] At every time and in every way imposing speech, with the spell it throws over us, prevails over that which aims at persuasion and gratification. Our persuasions we can usually control, but the influences of the sublime bring power and irresistible might to bear, and reign supreme over every hearer."[19]

Longinian sublimity at root is a form of possession made possible by the trace presence of the divine in the human. The potential for sublimely powerful moving expression exists differently among members of the species, but where it appears, it requires proper training (*techné*) and always has the species' perfection as its aim and its basis. It rests on and aspires to *arête* or human honor in the sense that Quintilian gives the notion, which he discusses under the figure *vir bonus dicendi peritus* ("the good man skilled in speaking"). Eloquence's sublime power can cause irrational actions and their consequences, yet its role in the species' self-creation as historical actor and in the creation of the human world as historical — this is something criticism and poetry insist upon as the alternative to barbarism and anomie.

In Vico, too, eloquence is the goal and means of education and the eloquent man is not only moral but also poetic and critical. Vico's anti-Cartesianism concludes "that the geometrical method constitutes a hindrance in the way of an eloquent exposition of the principles of physics" — a claim that hinders the social, political, and imaginative formation of what Vico calls here, "the multitude" (*SM* 24). Moreover and equally important, modern philosophy's decision to advance analytic method against the inheritance of poetry and criticism destroys entire fields of human possibility. Rather than supplement eloquence with analysis as classical philosophers had done in arranging the relations between mathematics and the republic of letters, the philosophical movements against eloquence destroys the very capacity for eloquence. Not only does analysis break the necessary pedagogical and thoughtful linkages between telos and means that eloquence should be, but also it reduces the very capacity of humans to be eloquent and, in that very movement, changes the nature of the human from its achieved status as historical to an arrested formation confident in its univocal and monocular imperial certainties.

What follows, ironically for the philosophers, is precisely that division between philosophers and the people that so preoccupied Pascal and which neo-conservatives reassert as the means of political control, as a desired political ideology. Those who worry about the dire effects of eloquence upon human emotion and motive lend their support, perhaps too readily, to the analytic ideal and so separate the philosophers into a domain of secure leadership — echoing Plato, of course — and in so doing sever the republican or democratic liaison produced between speakers and hearers in a domain of eloquence. The analytic worry that real world corruption and "unconscious drives" can abuse eloquence for evil purposes leads even putative democrats to the educational ideals of elitism, of the fit few who rule masses no better educated than they must be to need the ameliorative satisfactions of barbaric irrationalities provided by such things as consumerism and religion.

In an age of intense media saturation and corporate, party, and government control of images and their circulation, eloquence might well seem an irrelevant aspect of education or politics. Indeed, the succession of Papal and then Austrian imperial control over Naples created a similar circumstance in which citizens of a republic lost control of the signifying systems essential to their culture's elaboration. As Vico put it, "It may be objected that the form of government under which we live at present no longer allows eloquence to exercise its control over free peoples" (*SM* 39). Vico not only courageously acknowledges a dangerous centralization of power but a conformist, compliant, if not fearful attitude among the educated who cede autonomy and effort to that power in advance of any effort to make use of those opportunities that remain open to them to be intelligent and eloquent. Vico does find cracks in the authoritarian control exercised by emperors. He meant this early in his talk when he said that philosophers like Bacon and Descartes would accomplish more totally a control that sovereigns could only dream. "To which I answer," Vico said, "that we ought to be thankful to our monarchs for governing us not by fist but by laws." No matter how ironic this comment might be, it turns Vico's argument in an active political dimension that recognizes many public places for eloquent performance. "However, even under the republican form of government, orators have gained distinction by their fluent, broad, impassioned style of delivery in the law courts, the assemblies, and the religious convocations, to the greatest advantages of the state, and to the signal enrichment of the language" (*SM* 39). This strong echo of Dante's argument for the creation of a vernacular answers those moderns who say that eloquence belonged to heroic pre-republican forms. It answers as well all conformists who find no space for eloquence in imperial rule. Law, for Vico the basic institutional reflection of human poesis, assures the possibility of eloquent performance and with other public institutions demands the education of orators whose achievements in "enriching the language" mark their essential role in any thriving polity, in the historical development of the species. We might say that over and against both the dangers of imperial domination — especially the closing down of performative spaces in which eloquence, the practice of language by men made "good" by art and nature, might display its formative value.

Vico's complex affection for Plato appears in his account of the means by which eloquence does its work upon an audience: "an orator is persuasive when he calls forth in his hearers the mood which he desires . . . the soul must be enticed by corporeal images and impelled to love; for once it loves, the fire of passion must be infused into it so as to break its inertia and force it to *will*" (*SM* 38). The soul is not the terrain of reason but passion and love. Eloquence is the name for that which activates will over against inertia. Without will, there is neither resistance nor creation. It is easy to see how the species requires eloquence if it is to complete the lacunae in its culture, if it is to elaborate itself under the leadership of the sage poet whose privilege is talented and trained goodness.

While Vico is not a perfectionist in his understanding of the human species, he is an historicist who believes in the evolution of the species into its historicality as the consequent potential of its own complex structure as learning, willing, and self-motivating being. Whatever is might not be necessary, because it is human and historical; but among those things that exist is the human, itself in its historical potentiality for willful action. Inertia is not, for Vico, tradition but conformity, the loss of will, the only seemingly paradoxical result of tyranny and imperial ambition. These all effectively erase the very potentiality for poesis that is the highest human quality. The human is always a struggle, an agon that might appear as a psychomachia between the inert — and its violent political, intellectual forms — and the self-motivated will of the human's love for its own creative potentialities. Education is the means to assure the latter's survival, to identify its value, and to materialize its existence within the very minds and bodies of human beings. It is not the only means — not if by education we mean only schooling — but even as schooling, as training in the intersection between technique and honor (*techné* and *arête*), then it is essential.

Of course, its opposite has many names and comes in the form of many practices. For Vico, some of these, as we have seen, are analytic philosophy and imperial knowledge systems. Another name for creativity's anti-historical and anti-human enemy is torture, a topic to which we will turn increasingly as these lectures progress. I want to end this lecture, however, with the discussion of one moment that relates eloquence to torture explicitly and does so precisely in the context of early modern science's ambitions and Christianity's response.

John Wesley was a younger contemporary of Vico who lived from 1703 to 1791. In 1957, the British psychiatrist William Walters Sargant praised Wesley for having fortified the English against the materialistic temptations that came to their cruel apex in the French Revolution. Why does this matter here? Sargant's praise appears in an important and controversial book, *Battle for the Mind: A Physiology of Conversion and Brainwashing*,[20] that is necessary reading for anyone interested in the sciences of mind, mind control, and personality repair or disruption. Sargant worked with trauma patients during and after the Second World War and his work influenced many readers. G. Seaborn Jones, in his book *Treatment or Torture*,[21] offers this useful summary of Sargant's work:

> We are reminded of one of the crucial conclusions of this book. In *Battle for the Mind* conceptual analysis is carried to the point where it becomes clear that any profound reorientation of thought, such as conversion to

or from a religion or political ideology, is not purely intellectual, but has
an affective basis which requires a psychodynamic explanation.[22]

This apparent truism reminds us, of course, of Longinus and Vico, especially
the latter's insistence that eloquence moves the passions to will through love.
Curiously, this brain scientist had discovered the truth Vico reiterated that
minds, all minds, including elite minds of trained scientists — all minds change
profoundly not through analytic argument alone. All profound belief changes
require affective involvement. This places the issues of human formation squarely
back on the terrain of classical eloquence, of Vichian figurations of historical
humanism, and most important posits a conflict between brain scientists and
humanistic critics for authority and legitimacy in the shaping of humans, the
species, and the educational systems of values and techniques upon which, in
part, cultured societies rest.

Seaborn Jones's study of Sargant's work falls within a larger analysis of
the relation between psychiatry, and neurology, and torture. What the scientists
learned is not contestable. Seaborn Jones criticizes Sargant for hypocrisy and
violence against the human subject that not only is a perverse result of his
science but also has mere national ideology as its legitimation. Sargant's praise
of Wesley shows Seaborn Jones that "although Sargant disapproves of the
techniques of brainwashing and indoctrination as used by foreign powers, he
admires Wesley's 'great success' with methods he finds very similar, because
they were good for England!"[23] We might or might not share the political content
of this complaint. More interesting by far is Sargant's method and discovery.

Sargant admired Wesley not merely for the effect his movement had in
making Britain a popular bastion against the shocks of Paris in 1789. He learned
something from Wesley that belonged to his own research field: "terrifying
eloquence" can be equivalent to "brainwashing and indoctrination" precisely in
its impact upon affect so that profound changes might take place in the human
subject. "It is now generally admitted," Sargant wrote in 1957, "that [Wesley]
made great numbers of ordinary English people think less about their material
well-being than their spiritual salvation, thus fortifying them, at a critical period
of the French Revolution, against dangerous materialistic teachings of Tom
Paine."[24] Indeed, in a celebratory apostrophe that should make all secularists
shudder with horror, Sargant concludes that advanced brain science is no threat
to religion because preachers, scientists, and politicians can and should rearrange
minds and brains to support Christian values, cultural practices, and socio-
political acts and institutions. "Must a new concentration on brain physiology

and brain mechanics weaken religious faith and beliefs? On the contrary, a better understanding of the means of creating and consolidating faith will enable religious bodies to expand much more rapidly."[25] If historical evidence must supplement laboratory work, then Wesley's eloquence is enough and Sargant's work opens the door both to the alignment between brain studies and torture and to the competition between those imperial, analytic forces and the poetic humanism of Vico's historicism. This intellectual development has implications beyond the idea of manufacturing consent. Neuroscience teaches us that the brain is malleable and that experience changes its physical capacities, creating and removing pathways of memory and cognition.[26] Criticism should realize that it must play on these largest fields of human endeavor. It must embrace the proper aim. If it does not, it leaves those fields to others whose ethics do not, like Quintilian's, insist that a "good man" be both the end and foundation of human will. We will later see how J.S. Mill contributes to our history and our armory as critics in these struggles.

3
Erich Auerbach and Invention of Man

There are at least two different ways to introduce Erich Auerbach following what we have said about Vico. On the one hand, we might speak of him as a scholar who embraces philology as a method for thinking about literature and culture because it recognizes that human being is a self-making historical species — and so we might begin with a look at philology. On the other hand, we might approach Auerbach as a reader and student of Vico, about whose work he thought long and seriously, writing essays that give us perhaps the best literary critical understanding we have of the Italian's work and historicism's value to criticism and culture. These approaches converge, of course, linking great literary scholars across national boundaries and historical epochs; they converge at a point of great discovery of what I call the invention of the human.

Much of what I say today focuses on one chapter in Auerbach's greatest and most influential book, *Mimesis: The Representation of Reality in Western Literature*.[1] *Mimesis* is so well-known and so much written about that I introduce it only by saying that its author was a romance philologist by training, a fact that I interpret as politically significant — that is, as importantly different from either Germanic or classical philologies that might well have become more easily part of the official culture of Nazism. Auerbach was also a Jew who fled for his life to Turkey where, as he says in "The Epilogue," he wrote this book without the resources of a major research library, but with the support of a Papal Nuncio who allowed him access to the Vatican library in Istanbul.

Mimesis comes into the world marked with all the richness that study, exile, and experiential complexity might produce. It exists in part because of cultures' mutual interpenetration: writing at the eastern end of the Mediterranean, this specialist in romance languages and literature makes use of a Catholic institution in a then insistently secularized Turkey to write a book that "Christian Europe," by his torture and killing, would have made impossible. *Mimesis* sits before its readers as a cry of conscience against those intellectuals, specialists, and politicians who repudiate the interactions of cultures and institutions and treat them violently, reductively, in terms of simple national, bordered, or linguistic identities. The grandeur of Auerbach's achievement is the preemptive indictment specifically of all those who entice or enable power with monologic stories about nations, languages, and cultures and who forget what Vico and Auerbach certainly knew: the intellectuals' task is to reinforce the pollinating, fertile, and interesting richness of common human life lived and thought differently but compassionately, empathetically, with love.

I intend to discuss Auerbach's reading of Dante, especially his discussion of *The Inferno*, the first part of Dante's great Italian poem, *La Commedia*, which tells the story of the poet's descent into hell with the Roman poet, Virgil, as his guide. I will comment mostly on the chapter entitled, "Farinata and Cavalcante," about which I will say more as we go along.[2] I want to draw your attention to one specific but crucial moment in this essay and from it, follow the lines of interest that appear. I commend this as one of the most daring moments in critical history, a moment when a great critic, reading an even greater poet, finds the truth that humanity is a poetic creation — that poetry created modern humanity, and this because of the historical development of the species' cultural capacities.

In the tenth canto of *The Inferno*, as Virgil and Dante discuss the condemnation of heretics and atheists, a Tuscan voice arises from the tombs, hailing Dante the Pilgrim, stopping him in his passage. At the very start of his readings, Auerbach insists that we acknowledge the difficult greatness and grand originality of this poetry. His comments are always comparative and in this case, he raises Dante against a background of great writings he has already studied — the Homeric epics, the Hebraic Bible, the Song of Roland, and other major classical and medieval texts. Comparative critical technique permits both evaluative and historical placement of Dante's work. "More is packed together in this passage," writes Auerbach, "than in any of the others we have so far discussed in this book; but there is not only more, the material is not only weightier and more dramatic within so short a space; it is also intrinsically much more varied" (178). Density, complexity, dramatic seriousness, and variety — these are the literary qualities Auerbach embraces as the highest achievement and propounds as a specific nexus of ethical-historical awareness of human richness and possibility. These qualities are neither random anachronistic judgments of personal taste nor reflections of twentieth-century ideology. Rather they embody a critical historical consciousness of the coalescence of style and history, of value and achievement.

We need to read this moment with some care. The subtitle of *Mimesis, Representations of Reality in Western Literature*, encourages a first reading of Auerbach's remark as praise for Dante's ability to represent, to present again and for us, an already existing, increasingly complex modernizing Western world. This first reading requires a supplement. Auerbach's use of the term, "dramatic," is our first key to this need. Drama, as we recall, means action or performance; it means to do. What is dramatic about Dante's lines is what they do, the fact that they do. This is Auerbach's point: in this scene Dante's writing is relational, marked by sudden changes of direction, by interruption — qualities that do not cause a collapse into formlessness or distraction but that exist in a new structure that is not only situational, that is, contextualized, but "a concomitant of the structure of the Comedy as a whole" (178). In Vico's sense, Dante's poetry is the metaphoric action of acute perception. The poetry is dramatic as an account of action, but more important and fundamentally, as performance, it is action; it achieves effect. As representation, it brings into being the complex, varied relationalities that are human life — lived in modern contexts, set in depths, caught in light and shadows, bearing its own past, its own complex of intertwined experiences that come from different people, sometimes in conflict, living together, crossing each others' paths.

Auerbach's critical technique analyzes how literary styles achieve reality effects. Discussing this moment in canto ten, he shows how the "rapid succession of independent episodes or mutually unrelated scenes" coalesces into a unity through "an abundance of syntactic connectives." He also shows that in more extreme cases of discontinuity, where syntax alone cannot create liaisons between merely juxtaposed scenes that have "sharp contours without transition" — he shows that Dante's structural and expressive invention managed these "confrontation[s] . . . by means of artistically varied devices of expression which are rather changes of approach rather than parataxis" (178). The point about not using parataxis is important. Hebraic texts relied on parataxis and Auerbach knew Homeric instances of the device. We might remember Latin classroom texts insisting that Julius Caesar's *Gallic Wars* began with the most famous instance of parataxis in Western literature. That Dante's poetry achieved relations among more and more complex elements and at a deeper, more coherent level than the classics or Bible could manage — this was an historically critical point for laying out the key role literature has in creating the very creature we came to know as the human. It is as if the time were ripe for literary invention and that the ripeness was the complex reality created by the emerging complexities of culture, trade, and thought that resulted from the increased cross-border and cross-language fertilizations that enriched the Italian city-states.

Auerbach is not, however, a deterministic historicist. Dante's invention is no more caused or dictated by the necessities of its time than it was free of the conditions that gave it free play, a field in which to act historically. As Auerbach describes Dante's stylistic success, he also portrays those historical qualities of his art's conditions and nature. We see this very clearly as he concludes his description of Dante's historical primacy and poetic uniqueness. "The scenes," Auerbach writes, "are not set stiffly side by side and in the same key — we are thinking of the Latin legend of Alexis and even of the *Chanson de Roland* — they rise from the depths as particular forms of the momentarily prevailing tonality and stand in contrapuntal relation to one another" (178).

What does it matter that Auerbach uses musical metaphors to describe Dante's stylistic and visionary accomplishment? That he insists that Dante is best described as contrapuntal rather than paratactic? Poetry is music, tradition tells us; so Auerbach's choice seems unremarkable. Yet, that he emphatically denies Dante's style is paratactic while insisting it is contrapuntal is too interesting for us to ignore. Edward Said made the claim that all good criticism, like all culture, is contrapuntal, but rather than leap to Said's theory we should first consider what it is about Dante that Auerbach designates with the term.

Historically, Western music has since the seventeenth century understood itself in terms of "keys," as harmonic. Auerbach defines the rhetorical device, parataxis, as a standing stiffly side by side, in the same unvarying key. The first part of this definition recalls a minor element in the etymology (or better, philology) of a common Greek and military usage of parataxis to designate military formation, as in the phalanx. Whatever else we might say about Dante's complex style, it does not move (or hold its ground) as if it were a phalanx. The shift to musical terms is also a shift within musical terms, from a plain chant of one key to a modern compositional mode that has a key signature that allows internal tonal modulation. Dante, Auerbach claims, is writing a modern style; variations within and between scenes result from shifting relations among "momentarily" dominant tonalities — in other words, as with modern Western music in general — the poem gravitates toward its major key.

Readers easily interpret Dante's "major key" as the expressive and structural equivalent of the godhead. Auerbach's critical courage, his historical daring, is to refuse this ready interpretation and make the historicality of the human the dominant key toward and out of which minor movements, passing events, alignments among such events gravitate. Momentary tonalities rise from the depths as particular forms that that tonality might take. It would be hard for Auerbach to emphasize more the transitory nature of these scenes and events: particulars as manifestations of the momentary. What matters, of course, is not only that but also how these stand in relation to each other, forming something that stabilizes their particularity and, indeed, even reveals something of that from which these all arise.

Modern counterpoint starts, and some might say ends, with Bach, so exhaustive were his experiments in musical elaboration. Like Dante, of course, Bach built his most impressive aesthetic artifacts on genre, conventions, and histories that were institutionally and affectively religious. His great "Mass in B Minor" is only the most outstanding example. Christoph Wolff's "life history" of Bach explains the composer's oeuvre, career, and thought as a tightly integrated exploration of the most profound connections between art, human life, the universe, and God.[3] Dante's life had much more of an explicitly political component to it — so much so that we know he took revenge on his political opponents by placing them carefully in hell — but on the surface it seems as closely woven a unit of thought and art as Bach's. We have a good deal of license to use Bach to illuminate the secularized German Auerbach's characterization of Dante's emerging poetic modernity as contrapuntal. We must first give some brief sense of Bach's own invention and intent in working with counterpoint.

Bach inherited a Renaissance music that had its own contrapuntal techniques. The madrigal, for instance, mixed homophony with the imitative counterpoint common in the period.[4] According to Auerbach, however, Dante's counterpoint is far in advance of the madrigal or other contemporary musical forms. Like the later Bach, Dante structures his counterpoint simultaneously and complexly along both vertical and horizontal axes — "depths" and "prevailing tonalities."

If we turn to Wolff's authoritative explication of Bach's technique, we find the illumination we need. Wolff contends that to understand Bach's achievements requires a grasp of Bach's interest in and experiments with the fugue. Put simply, Bach showed the fugue to be the form that best allows the exploration of musical thought. Because the fugue's structural demands and elasticity required mastery of counterpoint's principles to work within its capacities, Bach's genius gave itself to expositing them fully. "From the beginning," Wolff writes, "Bach savored the challenge of formulating a musical thought that would not just provide the raw material for a musical structure but that would define the shape of its individual voices, their interaction, the progress of the piece, and finally the character of the whole" (93). This sentence is an exact gloss on Dante's use of counterpoint in the tenth canto. Unlike in imitative counterpoint, Bach's style made the voices "individual" while their juxtaposition — their vertical interaction, as it were — combined with their horizontal movement, their elaboration, to form a progress, the temporality of which is essential. As far as this style provides the "character of the whole," it is what we in literary studies sometimes refer to as the work's vision — on the basic assumption that form and content, style and insight are one. To say that Bach or Dante's vision is contrapuntal is to say too little and too much but we must risk this confusion to make clear that much can ride on what might seem like a minor and passing moment in Auerbach's long and magisterial study.

An heir of Bach — who was a near contemporary of Vico — Auerbach (unlike Bach, not a Protestant) would have known how daring it was anachronistically to apply this notion to Dante, and his doing so suggests not only Dante's profound creation of human historicism but Auerbach's equally deep commitment to sustain its emergence within the species' historicality. There is no surprise in noting Auerbach's commitment, especially given his admiring writings on Vico's historism. I find nothing surprising either in his desire to find a great predecessor for his own position in Dante. When I say his own position, I mean both his modern historism and his humanistic commitment to the secular historical nature of the species in culture. Dante's contrapuntal style is Auerbach's chosen example of and name for this combination of poetic invention and critical responsibility. Criticism has both the capacity and the obligation to treat itself seriously, to preserve its capacities and ethics as part of the historical project of humanity's work to perfect its cultural capacities and build futures.

Dante is the name Auerbach gives that moment when the species emerged in its conscious humanity as the self-creating species, aware not only — à la Descartes — of its own consciousness, but of its own social, cultural, and historical existence as fully historical, even if, in Marx's infamous phrase, men "do not make [history] exactly as they please."[5] The historical achievement of an art that complexly builds progress and structure from a style that moves along two axes simultaneously — this is a species achievement. Critical historicism has the ethical obligation to hold this truth as an axiom and to insist that it must be axiomatic in all critical practices that take the species and its artistic, political, and intellectual components as objects of careful study. In other words, what emerges upon Dante's historical, aesthetic invention is an ethical critical obligation to the species' historicality and its existence as an agent that must not regress from this accomplishment. Auerbach creates for himself and leaves for his readers not only literature's essential function in creating the species' historicality but the obligations this imposes upon criticism, obligations that far exceed in gravity any other criteria for its practice or success.

Bach made counterpoint a device for the most profound intellectual work, or more exactly, as with so much else that Bach did, he took counterpoint as he found it and explored it, elaborated it, nearly completing the articulation of its capacities to enable thinking in music. His genius knew that counterpoint had the capacities needed to extend his thinking about fundamental questions such as, to quote Wolff, "what was possible in art." In pieces like *Trias harmonica*, Wolff argues, Bach "captures" and masters time, space, and their "complex interrelationship," to the extent that we can perform the piece forward and backward; in this composition, Bach addressed the fact that time is both progressive and regressive. His style was "a true mirror of the well-ordered universe," a device for reflecting and creating the ultimate reality, godhead and its universe:

> Bach's concentrated approach to his work, to reach what was possible in art, pertained to all aspects of music, from theory to composition and from performance to physiology and the technology of instruments. In the final analysis, this approach provides the key to understanding his never-ending musical empiricism, which deliberately tied theoretical knowledge to practical experience. Most notably, Bach's compositions, as the exceedingly careful musical elaborations that they are, may epitomize nothing less than the difficult task of finding for himself an argument for the existence of God — perhaps the ultimate goal of his musical science. (337–39)

Bach is no Cartesian. In Vico's term, he ties experience to theory. Rather than analyze, he explores and exploits the eloquent potential of musical topoi. In the terms of my first lecture on Vico, we would say that Bach was not a pioneer but a prospector: "One of his study methods," Wolff explains, "consisted of taking a given model and turning it into a new work. . . . And in the process of recomposing, he discovered new thematic connections or contrapuntal combinations as well as new harmonic, melodic, and rhythmic features." What Bach created in his eloquent elaboration on musical commonplaces was "a new solution to what he took to be a musical question" (93). His career shows us how much relentless hard work historical and secular humanity does and must put into the tasks of thinking, knowing, living, and creating capacities for others in the present now and coming in our futures — if, that is, the present manages to leave its heirs the capacity to imagine and create them.

Dante's counterpoint would be to the naïve historicist anachronistic and impossible. The fault lies in a contextualism that imagines poetic intelligence incapable of creativity that supplements, redirects, and exploits the potentialities it inherits, finds waiting, or invents. Auerbach's historism is, like Vico's, specifically aesthetic; it shares in the poesis of all creativity, that is, the ability to make something new of the topoi it encounters. This is a claim that Auerbach's courage makes possible for all humanistic historists. Like all eloquence, art (and criticism) knows its materials as Bach knew his exercises and tunes, as Dante knew his Virgil. Like eloquence, infused with, dependent upon, and aiming at creativity, art (and criticism) sustains what it inherits often by drawing from its depths resources not yet examined and it prospectively aligns those resources with futures that it is our responsibility to imagine if not incarnate.

A deterministic contextualism that would grant the agent nothing but what seeming context and seeming inheritance "allow" — this is the unethical interruption of the species' creativity and its historical existence as a creator of and dweller in cultures. Art (and criticism) set out from a contrapuntal position and so never accept the singularity of an all-encompassing, restrictive economy of signification, of socio-political or psychological potential. The unethical nature of the all-knowing determinist who makes private drama of minor struggles and offers that as public necessity — that lack of ethics destroys criticism, art, and poesis as the bases upon which the species creates itself as historical and in history. Such naïve determinists, such minor players in the private fantasies of their own minimalism, are merely the necromantic allies of those analysts whose commitment to necessary ignorance merely completes, as Vico told us, the worst ambitions of unjust sovereignty and imperial ambition.

The key signature to Bach's oeuvre is C-major, the C-major triad being "the only truly perfect chordal harmony," because "it is this sound that symbolized the dogma of the Holy Trinity. Like no other combination of tones, the natural triad could make audible and believable . . . the triad of perfection and [God-] likeness . . . the abstract 'image of divine perfection,' and at the same time, the essential identity between the Creator and the universe" (338). The key signature to Dante is "man" and all the modulations, variations, and elaborations in the structured process of the *Comedy* gravitate toward its representation and creation, toward an understanding of its place in as well as difference from the universe of which it seems to be the conscious and creative part.

I have spoken of Auerbach's daring on more than one occasion. I insist that critics must take daring to be axiomatic. If we recall Vico's insistence on the importance of metaphor over analysis as the drawing of acute lines, then we have some sense of Auerbach's method and ambition. Adhering closely to the text, in the way that Bach adheres closely to the opening theme of *The Goldberg*

Variations, Auerbach empirically records aspects of style and aligns them with literary historical and poetic effect. Auerbach in this gesture is an exemplum of our common ethical obligation.

Dante's counterpoint anticipates Bach's (seemingly) metaphysical artistic purpose. As Auerbach puts it following his discussion of Farinata and Cavalcante, Dante's style demonstrates his "basic conception of the individual in this world and in the world beyond. The character and function of a human being have a specified place in God's idea of order, as it is figured on earth and fulfilled in the beyond"(197). Bach and Dante come together around a desire to know and demonstrate God's order and the individual's place within it. What Auerbach establishes, however, is that Dante's art creates the individual, the modern human subject, that is part of his and Bach's cosmic sense of things. For Bach the Protestant, this relation demands a private if aesthetically performable demonstration of God's existence and man's proper adoring worship. For Dante the Catholic, the plurality of the human as a species being requires a modern account of the human as individual. Better than account, we should say it requires a representation of the human as individual precisely in the complex integrated historicality of a creature that exists on the two axes of alignment and progress.

To put the matter bluntly, Auerbach reads Dante as producing, for the first time, the human, itself. That this is "the first time" is easy to demonstrate and evidence exists in two simple things. Auerbach was a profoundly discriminating scholar who wrote carefully and understood the full historical and cultural gravity implied by great critics' precision. We should offer him the same respect as he gives other writers' care. For example, he notes that "many important critics" disliked or were uneasy with Dante's mixing of styles, of the low mimetic and sublime modes. The sublime, of course, suits the matter of divinity, of Virgilian precedence, and Dante's visionary ambition. The low mimetic, the recording of the mundane and transient details of life, sin, and society that persist in creating characters even in their after-life — the low mimetic contradicts classical aspirations to purity of style. Goethe, Auerbach records, described Dante's "closeness to the actual in the realm of the sublime" as "his 'repulsive and often disgusting greatness'" (185). Of course, Auerbach had prepared the ground for clarifying and correcting Goethe's judgment by noting that Dante's style is neither monologic nor paratactic. This description accepts the critics' perception but refutes their objections with more precise historicist readings of Dante's style.

Auerbach reminds his readers that Dante was not the first to mix styles. The medieval Christian drama, to take only one instance, exemplified what critics, including the so-called humanists — those committed to classicism's rigorous rules of order — thought was the naïveté of the unsophisticated. No one, however, Auerbach points out, could ever accuse Dante of naïveté. His evident high seriousness, his eloquence, invention, and ethical rigor demand respect and once acknowledged challenge his critics' judgments seemingly forever. More to the point, however, Auerbach's entire reading of Dante accounts for his achievement in terms of historical literary originality from an historical perspective that the critics, including Goethe, did not possess. Of course, Dante had a tremendous aesthetic capacity that Auerbach calls by the term, power — "Dante's powerful temperament." The contextualizing reductionist would analyze away the quality Auerbach alludes to with this figure. The "classicists" and others who object to the mixture of styles were unable to appreciate the fullness of Dante's originality because unlike Auerbach they were not able to see it from the vantage point of its disappearance. As we shall see in a few moments, when we turn to the end of *Mimesis*, Auerbach worried that the literary invention of the human and the ethical responsibility to historical humanism might disappear in late modernity, a moment that embodied sufficient change in humanity's development that its own historical existence, its own self-achievement, were at risk. Since Auerbach is a comparatist — a point that we must always stress — and since his comparisons, like Vico's, crossed time as much if not more than nations and languages, modernity's trajectory illuminated Dante's importance to a degree that Auerbach's predecessors would have had trouble understanding. Ironically, Auerbach appears as something of an emblem of the anxiety of Dante's humanism, late in the history of historicism's literary emergence. That lateness does allow, however, Auerbach great clarity about the depth and value of Dante's accomplishment.

Auerbach must establish at least two things about Dante. First, he must describe the nature of Dante's originality as an initiatory capacity to inherit and transform. Second, he must produce a reading of Dante as the literary achievement that brought man as historical agent into being, into full relief. Combining Dante the powerfully originating poet with the high accomplishment of his art would give flesh to Auerbach's historical claims. As readers of Auerbach, we must resist the temptation to follow only the large contrails of his historical arguments. In the fine detail of his work, as he claims to be true of poets' styles, lays most of what interest us. From the passing mention of counterpoint, we follow Auerbach to Dante's use of the vocative in the tenth canto.

As Virgil leads Dante the pilgrim through hell, his compatriot, the deceased Farinata, rises from his tomb and cries out, "*O Tosco, che per la città del foco vivo ten vai.*" ("Oh Tuscan, who go alive through the city of fire."[6]) Following Vico, I have argued that criticism must be comparative, historicist, and philologically attentive if it hopes ever to acquire the historical consciousness of human possibility that this passage contains and that Auerbach's reading illustrates. Only the comparative philologist is the critical match to originary poetry of such a kind:

> This is an address, a vocative introduced by O, with a succeeding relative clause which, in comparison with the vocative, is decidedly weighty and substantial; and only then comes the request, which is again weighted down with reserved courtesy. . . . The construction, "O thou who" is extremely solemn and comes from the elevated style of the antique epic. Dante's ear remembers its cadence as it remembers so many other things in Virgil, Lucan, and Statius. I do not think the construction occurs before this in any medieval vernacular. (179)

Auerbach no doubt remembers Dante's insistence on the role the library plays in the formation of vernacular languages, especially for Italy, which lacked a national sovereign and court system. Reading and study play on the body, internalized to the point that the body knows without the mind's direction to recollect. Mind and body are one as experience and knowledge coalesce. "Dante's ear remembers." At this level of poetic invention mastery is more than what consciousness directs and it is the result of the long hard work required to shape the mind and body as the elaboration of one's own will and of those whose works one encounters, inhabits, and hosts.

Dante's originality is in the transformation, the carrying over from one place where he found it to another where it can live, of a rhetorical and poetic resource. Simply, there is a movement from Latin and grammar to the vernacular:

> But Dante uses it in his own way: with a strong adjuratory element — which is present in antiquity at most in prayers — and with so condensed a content in the relative clause as only he can manage. Farinata's feeling and attitude toward the passing pair [Dante and Virgil] are so dynamically epitomized in the three qualifiers, *per la città del foco ten vai, vivo, così parlando onesto*, that had the master Virgil really heard those words, he might well have been more dismayed than Dante in the poem; his own relative clauses after a vocative are perfectly beautiful and harmonious to be sure, but never so concise and arresting. (179)

We might read this passage in light of the dramatic and theological forces that situate Virgil: having lived before Christ, he cannot ascend to heaven and divine reward. Auerbach is, however, saying something more, namely that Dante's art transforms the theological dramatic into an historical poetic drama. In an agon of styles, Dante wins the glory of mastery over his teacher. This is not an individual or personal conquest of a poet facing a great predecessor. Psycho-personal anxieties are trivial. Dante advances beyond Virgil because he creates a fully individualized human figure, Farinata, who carries with him, even in death, all the marks of history, character formation, and socio-cultural specificity. In Dante's vocative, the modern human subject emerges historicized beyond the reach of Virgil's capability, of the status of the species in his imperial world.

Poetry creates the modern human subject as this particularized, individual, complex, and historical creature. Based on this reading, Auerbach discovers a profound ethical dimension with political overtones in Dante's aesthetic originality. Focused as he is on Dante's realistic portrayal of characters' full historical individuality even in hell, Auerbach insists — in one of his weaker moments, I think — on finding a history to hell itself. Recalling previous visits by Aeneas, Paul, and Jesus, Auerbach stresses that as part of his realism, Dante's hell has landscapes, events, populations — all the marks of a fully created world. More important, however, is the fact that Dante records the emerged historical human as that created by and represented in literature. Nothing less than what Dante does to position poetry as itself the emerged expression of the human's being as its own history — this is what matters to Auerbach.

Dante's invention is what produces the ethical demand upon criticism to care for the historical human as its first obligation and to care for literature's capacity as its second. Accustomed as we are to the categories of fantasy and the like, in books like *The Lord of the Rings* and films like *Star Wars* or the great cinematic achievements from Ophals to Guillermo del Toro, it might seem odd that we would call a narrative of hell "realistic." Of course, at least since Coleridge, we have the idea that realism is an effect of probability and consistency. Certainly, Dante pursues his givens with the full effect of realism.

It is this Auerbach strains to work out; he reads the breadth and depth of its significance. He starts with the oft-repeated point that Dante portrays characters realistically: "Their own earthly lives, then, they still possess completely, through their memories, although those lives are ended. . . . the impression they produce is not that they are dead — though that is what they are — but alive." Individuation takes the literary form of historical particularization and the devices are modern: characters have memories; passing time — experience, knowledge — makes them who they are and who they remain; their identities become "their own" in the process — individuals can claim themselves as their own, as their proper selves persistently self-identified, but with finite capacities or limits marked by death itself:

> Here we face the astounding paradox of what is called Dante's realism. Imitation of reality is imitation of the sensory experience of life on earth — among the most essential characteristics of which would seem to be its possessing a history, its changing and developing. Whatever degree of freedom the imitating artist may be granted in his work, he cannot be allowed to deprive reality of this characteristic, which is its very essence. (191)

What interests us here are two things: first, Auerbach's successful effort to describe the means by which Dante produces realism effects in an arena seemingly without human history, where characters have only pasts (memories) and no futures (anticipations); second, the historical consequences of Auerbach's discovery and the motives for it.

Auerbach does not claim that Dante can do what he would with hell since it exists as a human creation; this would be inappropriate to Dante's theological scheme, which determines these characters' place not only in a category of sinners but in a cosmological order. What at first seems like a structural and metaphysical impediment turns out to be the occasion for Dante's modern realism. Within each classification of sinner, within each venue of punishment, the individual characters' histories and personalities persist:

> as individuals of different personalities, of different lots in their former lives, and of different inclinations, they are most sharply contrasted . . . from the fact that earthly life has ceased so that it cannot change or grow, whereas the passions and inclinations which animated it still persist without ever being released in action, there results, as it were a tremendous concentration. We behold an intensified image of the essence of their being, fixed for all eternity in gigantic dimensions, behold it in a purity and distinctness which could never for one moment have been possible during their lives upon earth. (192)

It is as if Dante were discovering the full force and presence of human beings in their organized subjectivity. We might compare Dante's characters, as Auerbach sees them, with other Renaissance images of a similar kind; Rembrandt's self-portraits come immediately to mind. If we want to know what an individualized subject is, we would look as much to Dante's Farinata and Cavalcante as to Rembrandt's use of darkness and fine line to see how time passed marks human creatures as persons whose character, mind, and sensibility stabilize sufficiently to rest within a concentrated purity of expression. Death and damnation impose the conditions necessary for the human subject to stand forth, imaged as the product of sensibility, physiology, and experience. There might be no chance for future change, but these characters are clearly there in their rich and complex being, attractive to observation, available to understanding precisely because they have changed, have lived as fully historical creatures with a clear sense of their own temporal being, their own now-past involvement in history.

There are two consequences to Dante's art that matter to us, in these lectures on criticism and poetry. First is the uncovering of an ethical responsibility to the discovery that earthly sensibility possesses a changing and developing history. Second is the scholarly discovery of the continuing literary creation of that historical sensibility as a defining feature of modernity that modernity always threatens from within itself. The two together compel the writer and reader into the dual task of enhancing that discovery and continually evaluating its very possibility, its fitness in time.

Vico recognized a modern threat to historical humanism in the Cartesian analytic and its alignment with tyranny and imperialism. Auerbach's tragic knowledge that historical humanism had prevented neither the success of Nazism and its genocidal policies nor that of American-style mass culture led him to wonder if the literary were still an element in modernity that could preserve and enhance the humanist ideal. Moreover, modernist writings themselves — the works of Proust, Joyce, Woolf, and the like — seemed to him unlikely support for the ethical responsibility culture owed the emergent historical human. By the end of *Mimesis*, Auerbach considered these questions in terms that inverted the structural relations between literature and the emergent human in Dante. When writing on Woolf, for example, in whose *To the Lighthouse* he found the best materials for considering the success of humanism's project, Auerbach no longer believed that the critic could test literary writing's success by asking if it directly represented the increasingly historical complexity of the human. He had come to realize that the critic must ask a more modest-seeming question about a greater difficulty. Had the novel achieved the imaginatively more difficult but stylistically less grand effect of making the low mimetic, the quotidian, an important symbolic investment of private human meaning and affect? The answer to this question was a tentative yes. Sublime aspiration grounded Dante's mixture of styles; Goethe, for example, had no choice but to concede his greatness. Woolf, by contrast, sustains Dante's great inventions in the residual world of the personal from which it remains possible to create stories that both represent the sensibility as changing and developing and to do so in terms of that sensibility's involvement with objects and others in the historical world.

Since Auerbach ends *Mimesis* with considerable lament over the fate of historical humanism's richness, over the leveling effect that American modernism threatens to impose on the extraordinary variety of human life — thereby obliterating the capacity of life to vary — we have considerable reason to feel his strain in reading Woolf as a forceful heir of Dante. Nonetheless, Dante's discovery of an ethical responsibility persists in Woolf and in Auerbach's effort to read *To the Lighthouse* as a late form of modern historicism. Auerbach's lament at the fate of the human gains a great deal of its effect from the persistent ethical responsibility Dante's inventions imposed on readers and critics. In effect, Auerbach offers himself as a residual commonplace of a modernity that created and valued the human while at the same time constantly threatening to pass "beyond" it.

I want to leave you with a final point derived from Auerbach's great book, a principle of all critical attitudes. By the time Auerbach's historical account of literature and representation reaches the high moderns of the twentieth century, he has added an additional quality to his repertoire of judgments: love. He comes increasingly to associate literature's complex representations of human sensibilities as world with the qualities of love that authors feel for characters, characters for their worlds, and readers for what they can experience and think in encountering them all. Love and responsibility become one. Auerbach praises *To the Lighthouse* above most modernist experiments in form and aesthetics: "It is one of the few books of this type which are filled with good and genuine love" (552). What is the evidence for this? "What realistic depth is achieved in every individual occurrence!"

That exclamation mark is too interesting to let pass. It lends emphasis; it suggests surprise; it confirms possibility; it celebrates persistence and endurance; it announces the vitality of literature and the power of writing. Sadness also marks Woolf's novel, an accident that makes it fitting for Auerbach's ending. Love's parallel is "amorphous sadness." Both are achievements; both are historical markers of literature's fate and so that of the human. The two are inseparable.

Woolf's art is a clear development of and change to Dante's contrapuntal realism. *To the Lighthouse* puts "the emphasis on random occurrence, to exploit it not in the service of a planned continuity of action but in itself." Dante's structure was teleological, of course, so that the individualized subjects and their histories stood in place; about their historicality, nothing might be random. Characters belonged to the order of Dante's cosmological structure as they did to the grand historicality of their complexly interpenetrated political and domestic lives. If you will, as we have seen by following Auerbach's remarkable close reading of Dante, nothing was random. Poetry as plot action, as drama, had determined each reality's place in purpose. In Woolf's novel, the power of counterpoint to organize such deeply explored complexity yields to a generosity that does not compel the real into the service of action. As a result, Woolf's style creates new realisms and new forms of human subjectivity; Auerbach's ethical responsibility to the nexus of human history and realism enables, indeed, obliges his attention to these changes. Once more, we see that great criticism must be historically comparative. Auerbach explicitly compares Woolf to her contemporaries, but this entire passage rests on a historicized comparison with her greatest predecessors, as Dante's powerful individuality depended upon a successful comparison with his.

Woolf's strengths are not Dante's, nor could they be, but they are very considerable and they record, in their own way, the very strains within modernity that threaten to obliterate that human Dante created. Woolf is a great original and she too metaphorizes in Vico's sense. "Aspects of the occurrence" — Auerbach is writing about the stylistic effect of love — "come to the fore, and links to other occurrences, which, before this time, had hardly been sensed, which had never been clearly seen and attended to, and yet they are determining factors in our real lives." Action subsumes neither these occurrences nor their relations; consequently, her art achieves neither strongly individualized character nor order created along two axes, contrapuntally. The tolerant strength of Woolf's style is apophantic. Although it is also metaphoric and so seems by conjunction or acute perception to require the power of an ordering or contrapuntal ego, in fact, Woolf's achievement is to preserve the order of relation as essential to the judgment or discovery of what is. Since Woolf's realism puts no priority on action and allows each occurrence to be itself, it should not surprise Auerbach's readers that her art requires subsuming subjectivity within sensibility. Speaking of Woolf's strength in revealing the random, Auerbach adds that "in process something new and elemental appeared: nothing less than the wealth of reality and depth of life in every moment to which we surrender ourselves without prejudice." As we have learned from Auerbach already, when he speaks of something new appearing in the art, he means both that the art makes it appear and that this form of art is itself new and emerging. The judgment of novelty is, however, a weak apophantis but it leads to a moment of stronger judgment that is both ethical and historical and of the sort we find only in the work of great critics.

> To be sure, what happens in that moment — be it outer or inner processes — concerns in a very personal way the individuals who live in it, but it also (and for that very reason) concerns the elementary things which men in general have in common. It is precisely the random moment which is comparatively independent of the controversial and unstable orders over which men fight and despair; it passed unaffected by them, as daily life. The more it is exploited, the more the elementary things which our lives have in common come to light. The more numerous, varied, and simple the people are who appear as subjects of such random moments, the more effectively must what they have in common shine forth. In this unprejudiced and exploratory type of representation we cannot but see to what an extent — below the surface conflicts — the differences between men's ways of life and forms of thought have already lessened. (552)

Auerbach is exemplary in his abilities to be critically sympathetic, to move within the stylistic sphere of his great predecessors, like Dante and Woolf, and to remain enough distanced by the discipline of historical stylistics and philology to clarify as well as accumulate their achievements. Woolf's apophansis is the surrender of subjectivity so readers can judge the depth of life and the wealth of reality. Woolf's art does not repeat — cannot repeat — the power of counterpoint but substitutes for it a mode of surrender that makes the human something quite different from the highly detailed, densely sketched, one might even say arrested individualized subjectivity of Dante's characters or of Dante himself as poet. Poesis continues, however, in its historicality, making the human different from that created by the vocative and counterpoint. Auerbach's concern is always fundamental, that is, the relation between the literary and the human. He develops his comparative readings to the point of recognizing, in Woolf, that the achievement of literary humanism has exceeded its capacities which now not only cannot reverse but also actually contribute to the "leveling process" that threatens the values and achievements of historical humanism, itself. If Dante achieved variety and depth against the lock step of tight formation and a single key, modernism's experiments with the commonality of the human inherent in all diversity and variety smooths those over with "unification and simplification" (553).

"The strata of societies and their different ways of life have become inextricably mingled," Auerbach writes (552). Woolf's art makes the commonplace into the recognized realm of the commonly human. It joins and reflects large economic and cultural forces that, Auerbach fears, will eliminate variety and complexity and substitute simplicity. Auerbach ends with a rather odd combination of judgments, which Edward Said tried to disentangle.

Auerbach lived through some of modernity's worst disasters, especially the Nazi's destruction of European Jewry and the emergence of U.S.-style global mass culture. Having seen the tragedies that ensued upon the crack up of Dantean subjectivity and the confidence it once inspired, Auerbach was part of a small minority that regretted the passing of its virtues — diversity, richness, complexity, and pathos. Auerbach also traced and so intellectually lived through the history of the human's modern historical emergence and shattering. He had the critical responsibility to elucidate and narrate human potential and its shadows. What he saw, on both levels, he describes elegiacally: "So the complicated process of dissolution which led to fragmentation of the exterior action, to reflection of consciousness, and to stratification of time seems to be tending toward a very simple solution. Perhaps it will be too simple to please those who, despite all its dangers and catastrophes, admire and love our epoch for the sake of its abundance of life and the incomparable historical vantage point which it affords" (552–53).

Yet, *Mimesis* does not end on this note, but with an epilogue in which he speaks directly to his audience, to readers he hopes to find both among past friends, who may or not have survived the war, "as well as all the others for whom it was intended." Those readers would have to love in the way Auerbach and Woolf did, and they would have to have the capacities that Dante and his heirs enabled in Auerbach and other great humanistic critics. Such readers would learn to deal with "trends and tendencies" rather than fixed laws. They would have to learn to enjoy and value, "to accommodate multiplex data," and to produce "formulations correspondingly elastic" (556). Readers would have to have learned Woolf's lessons as well as Dante's, that is, to adhere to the random, as Auerbach chose to read randomly in his history and to follow his texts wherever they led him. That generosity within the achieved domains of human history was his greatest legacy to his readers. He hoped that his loving intention would create the readers his book needed and so allow him to do his part in preserving the ethical responsibility critics owe to history and to the human.

4
John Stuart Mill, *On Liberty* and Criticism

Is secular liberalism an ally of historical humanism's devotion to poetics and the defense of criticism? The question is too broad and our time too short to answer fully, but there is no doubt that Mill's great essay, *On Liberty*, published in 1859 — the same year as Darwin's *Origin of Species* and Marx's *A Contribution to the Critique of Political Economy* — gives us passionate and compelling reasons to think so. Moreover, in *On Liberty*, liberalism and historicism show themselves in some ways to be more than allies. Mill's liberalism is an important branch, an offshoot of the greater and more inclusive root of historical humanism. His devotion to individual freedom from obtrusive political and social authority emerges from the fact that in Western modernity humanity has become foundationally historical rather than fixed in its being. Historical humanity, to put it simply, has the capacities to develop itself as long as it remains historical. *On Liberty* is a defense of those abilities and a passionate warning against several threats to their existence, including, as Mill sees it, all forms of corporatist or collective authority that inevitably stifle freedom within conformity and error.[1]

On Liberty identifies not only those who would arrest the possibilities and necessity of historical transformation within repressive political regimes but others, especially intellectuals and their institutions that would deny the very fact of that historicality and so arrest the human within a natural concept that invariably accommodates itself to power and provides power with legitimating stories of human limitation. Mill's endorsement of the British Empire was inseparable from his thinking about liberty, believing as he did those British abilities to lead the world more likely assured the expansion of liberty he embraced. That Mill solidified the Empire's ideological self-justification is a brutal fact that shows how intertwined were the conditions of imperialism and the possibility of theorizing freedom. For all, although in different ways, these entanglements hopelessly but interestingly mar all liberal practices, institutions, and aspirations. Interest lies in how deeply Mill developed his thinking about liberty within the nexus of imperial culture that also reduced English life to mere commercialism, crude capitalism, and cultural closure. The horrors of that context, even if completely misjudged by Mill's embrace of the "Albion's Mission," make this essay a passionate and revealing reading of aspirations key to Western criticism.

In Mill — and this is the lesson we must learn from him in this set of lectures — criticism is the essential form that freedom takes to think and speak. Criticism is the *sine qua non* of historical humanity's struggle for itself and for the conditions of its own development.[2] *On Liberty* is an important imbuement of the historical human struggle against those tendencies of nature and power that would eradicate it, and Mill's pathos and urgency in defense of freedom — more important than any philosophical or analytic inconsistencies of theory — is a witness to achievement and an anxious anticipation of loss. It is this last that makes Mill our contemporary who can help us learn why and how to do literary criticism.[3]

Opponents on the political right and left have made us so suspicious of Mill's associations and philosophical lapses that to invoke him is to provoke a variety of passionate objections to his authority and example. Despite these circumstances, I want to do more than provoke; I want to reread *On Liberty* to remind us of the risks inherent in anti-liberalisms that either forget the achievements of liberalism or passionately oppose them. Mill is not, of course, the last or best word on matters of freedom and authority or of criticism and history, but his work highlights what we risk losing in any rush to deny the resources of liberalism — a rush that historically brings right and left into uncomfortable alliance. Liberalism is not the final word in that somehow "being in the middle" between extremes of right and left is not its position. On the contrary: liberalism's right-wing opponents, of whom I will say more later, would destroy those very institutions and values that its leftist antagonists frequently admire but find seriously limited. As far as many of those conservatives hostile to Mill are anti-democrats in contrast to those progressives who want, as it were, more democracy, we see how Mill's liberalism is not a middle path, a balance between extremes. Rather, Mill's conservative opponents are also, unlike his more progressive critics, likely to be anti-historicist, anti-secular, and anti-humanistic. They are likely to root themselves in natural law views of the world or in organicist ideals that resolve historical processes either into pseudo-Christian teleologies or into ideas of anarchy and anomie. Most important, they stand opposed to the centrality or indeed the possibility of criticism.

Postcolonial studies are one area in which many have written of "limits" in Mill: his work served the interests of colonialism if not racism and has left an irrefragable relation between liberalism and empire. Indeed, an expansive body of scholarship associated with postcolonialism's critique of European imperial culture has explicated his entanglements with and contributions to especially British domination of subaltern peoples.

In *Orientalism*, Edward Said establishes the framework for this postcolonial judgment and in three brief comments situates Mill and many of his contemporaries' work as parts of an imperial system they helped extend while producing important (if not always consistent) effects on British and Western culture and ideas. Others have added to what Said wrote, but he specified several paradoxes in Mill and other liberals' positions:

> It will not take a modern Victorian specialist long to admit that liberal cultural heroes like John Stuart Mill, Arnold, Carlyle, Newman, Macaulay, Ruskin, George Eliot, and even Dickens had definite views on race and imperialism, which are quite easily to be found at work in their writing. So even a specialist must deal with the knowledge that Mill, for example, made it clear in *On Liberty* and *Representative Government* that his views there could not be applied to India (he was an Indian Office functionary for a good deal of his life, after all), because the Indians were civilizationally, if not racially, inferior. The same kind of paradox is to be found in Marx.[4]

In fact, Mill's liberalism, aligned with other intellectual and religious movements, resulted in deregulation of imperial India and the imposition of rule through well-developed and well-legitimated liberal institutions such as a strong executive, "various legal and penal codes," and "a constantly refined knowledge of the Orient" (215). As Said argues — and I believe irrefutably — such knowledge production, the institutions that enabled it, and the aesthetic accomplishments that, in part, along with morality and economics, justified it — these together enforced a modernized version of "us" against "them":

> The human partnerships formed by reiterated cultural values excluded as much as they included. For every idea about "our" art . . . another link in the chain binding "us" together was formed while another outsider was banished. Even if this is always the result of such rhetoric, wherever and whenever it occurs, we must remember that for nineteenth-century Europe an imposing edifice of learning and culture was built, so to speak, in the face of actual outsiders (the colonies, the poor, the delinquent), whose role in the culture was to give definition to what *they* were constitutionally unsuited for. (228)

Postcolonial criticism sometimes has rather perversely extended Said's opinion to exclude Mill and others from serious consideration as resources for thinking by placing him within one rather grand counter-narrative of empire to the exclusion of other possible histories, other narratives that might allow supplementary views of his contributions to criticism. Of course, postcolonial scholars are not the only commentators on Mill. Anglo-American analytic philosophers of ethics and politics often refer to Mill, and they normally treat him without much if any reference to the colonial entanglements of his work. As I suggested in my earlier lectures comparing Vico to Descartes, this philosophy quarantines Mill and itself because analysts treat "philosophical" matters without reference to the world situation of the philosophers whose works they study or explicate. Such treatment is typical of the Cartesian ahistoricism that Vico opposed. Philosophers such as Rawls mention Mill only in the context of their efforts to "think" their own problems, in terms they believe belong to "philosophy," and not historically, as examples of human action with consequences in the world — that is, not in ways that would concern Said.

The most outstanding exception to this philosophical pattern is Isaiah Berlin, whose remarkable essay, "John Stuart Mill and the Ends of Life," deserves study by critics not only for the limits it reveals to others' philosophical methods of reading, but for its ability to bring the historicality of Mill as author into focus as a matter for political philosophy. While Berlin's purely conceptual analysis regrettably neglects what we call matters of style and expression, his interest in Mill as a writer, a thinker, and an historically engaged human agent, emphasizes Mill's passion and portrays his purposes as more important than any ill-refinement of concept or weakness in generalization. A single citation makes Berlin's case for Mill: "his voice is most his own when he describes the glories of individual freedom, or denounces whatever seeks to curtail or extinguish it."[5] (We will return to Berlin later in the talk.) Berlin admires the historicist conception of the human that Mill articulates and defends — despite the limitations of his understanding and theory — and wants to explain why societies and intellectuals should find Mill's passion attractive and necessary.

By contrast, right-wing ideologues, in economics, politics, and the human sciences, sometimes but at most grudgingly admire Mill for his arguments on behalf of freedom that seem to justify especially neo-liberal (or even libertarian) claims for the primacy of the market and private property. Yet such hesitant admirers at times object to Mill's social conscience, to his commitment to state involvement in education, regulation of social oppression by majorities, and so on. They worry about his criticisms of religion and the intent behind his secular humanism, which they sometimes align with "socialism." In effect, as in the title of a recent book, they worry that Mill intended to substitute "The Religion of Humanity" for Christianity or any organized form of monotheism.[6] *On Liberty* so clearly criticizes the threat religion poses to historical humanity that conservatives who insist on organized mass religion as a means of rule make the enormous conceptual leap of accusing Mill of socialism for his insistence on human and individual freedom from god and church.

The basic stories of Christianity — Protestant and Catholic — characterize human will as fallen, inadequate, in need of divine supplement. The long history of Christian debate over the relation between human will, divine will, salvation, and the necessity of acts of divine grace contains many careful distinctions. Mill's humanism, however, is relentlessly secular, uncompromising in his insistence that finite human will is honorable if imperfect, correctible by education, and formative of human ambition and ideals. Politics that deny the will such general value and democratic potential result in a repressive authoritarianism that either manipulates religious faith for early rule or denigrates all human efforts except those mysteriously "known" to reflect or represent god's supposed will. Mill illustrates his judgment of Christianity with the assertion that for Calvinism "the one great offense of man is self-will." Anti-democratic political elites generalize this position, even if they deny its applicability to themselves, with horrendous consequences for the emergent human: "capacities are withered and starved: they become incapable of any strong wishes or native pleasures, and are generally without either opinions or feelings of home growth, or properly their own" (68). In Mill's anthropology, religion is neither culture nor system, to adapt a phrase from Edward Said. Rather, religion is either the means for the diminution of the human in the shadow of what Christians call "the Final Days," or the demonic mechanism for authoritarian rule among those who cynically mistreat populations' need for meaning by offering rewards in other worlds.[7] In recent U.S. history, neo-conservative intellectuals have seemingly practiced such politics, especially as far as they appear to be heirs of Leo Strauss's disdain for democratic politics and popular will. The work of Strauss's most famous American student, Alan Bloom, who authored a book entitled, *The Closing of the American Mind*, is the most obvious example of this elitist politics extended to the domain of culture.[8]

Mill's conservative and neo-conservative antagonists would agree with Berlin that Mill was, despite his reputation for cold-hearted intellectualism, passionate about the subject of *On Liberty*. Unlike left-wing post-liberals' dismay over the limitations of Mill's awareness and his critical sense, these conservatives stridently object to Mill's great emphasis upon secular criticism as an essential element of free societies and as a marker of individuals' freedom to think and to form themselves within and when necessary against the oppression of state and social conformism. In effect, the reason Mill who was not a literary critic belongs in the history of our practice lies in his seemingly extramural, extraprofessional investment in criticism.

Criticism both emerges from and is essential to any continuing human ambition to perfect itself, or, in Vico's terms, to criticize, preserve, form and reform, or correct the inadequacies in our cultures as ways of living and thinking. Reading Mill makes illegitimate the ideology of academic professional indifference to literature and criticism's involvement in the world. It also reawakens our awareness of their roots in the essential task of Western modernity, namely, the historicization of the human, the ambition that imposes upon the human to aspire to its own perfection, and the struggle to preserve these possibilities from not only reactionaries but also contradictory forces within modernity itself. It restores criticism to its effective role in the historicization of humanity's anthropology. Perhaps because Mill was so much closer to the emergence of these possibilities than we were, he not only sensed their great civilizational values but their vulnerabilities in ways that our institutionalized professionalisms and our growing social attraction to the image do not allow.

I propose to address Mill's *On Liberty* as a text that exemplifies the force of critical thinking, which historical humanism and poetics justify. In other words, I suggest that we read Mill as an heir to Vico and a predecessor of Auerbach. Of course, Mill is very different from each of those critics, but in Coleridge's reading of *The New Science*, which began in 1825, we have an intermediating influence that brought Vico's thinking to bear on Mill's intellectual development. When Mill publishes his essay on Coleridge in 1840, having had by then considerable exposure to the poet, he describes Coleridge's beliefs in terms that we recognize as generally Vichian, as historical and humanist.

On Liberty is primarily about politics, ethics, and individualism; it is not primarily about aesthetics or historicism although both topics play a role in Mill's exposition of his position. Nevertheless, the account Mill gives of criticism makes his essay central to our topic and to our practice as literary and cultural critics.

Criticism is the exercise, not the deferral of judgment. In this, it is like training in the topoi, as Vico told his audience, elaborating a theory of education consistent with his own Ciceronian impulse toward the responsibility of citizens. It is an essential part of Mill's *On Liberty* that he closes with an insistence that freedom from state or corporatist control requires independent judgment, a capacious force to correct the will and actions of the state and other centralized powers. Properly organized societies — societies that produce freedom for dissenters as well as rigorous defenses of consensus — thrive only because they put in place the institutions and practices that enable independent judgment as an ideal and as a mode of life and thought. *On Liberty* famously ends with Mill warning against state organization of intelligence, of state appropriation of the "best minds," and against the inevitable inertia of collectivized judgment buttressed by its own allure. Individual freedom is the necessary alternative to this totalitarian or authoritarian outcome of modern social and political organization. The active means or embodiment of that possibility inheres, however, in freedom of judgment, intelligent powerful judgment that not only makes it possible for dissenters to choose and live different, independent forms of life, but that also challenge, undermine, and negate the agreed upon consensus and legitimating power of great collective forces. Hence, Mill's rhetorical stress in these lines from late in his essay: "It is indispensable, therefore, that the means should exist, independently of the government, of forming such ability, and furnishing it with the opportunities and experience necessary for correct judgment of great practical affairs."[9] Mill's knowledge of Tocqueville's books on America led him to claim that the United States is nearer the ideal condition for such possibilities than England or the European Continental powers — to say nothing of India or China. We might give Mill's complex vision simple expression: the social tendencies in which the development of independent judgment flourishes as a recognized condition of freedom and human resistance to modern forms of domination inherent in the state, in religion, and in the unquestioned dominance of the market. He brings himself to give his ideal of decentralized forms of democratic politics the name of "America" because at this point in his essay he feels he has to meet his readers' likely expectations and provide specific examples of the forms liberty might take. Until the final part of *On Liberty,* he has felt no compulsion to describe or exemplify alternative social and political structures to those his criticism exposes for their failures to sustain human historical possibility in its political and intellectual forms of freedom. Mill is reluctant to do this because he believes deeply in what he calls "negative criticism" (51).

Unlike Bentham, Mill practices a kind of "negative criticism" that is not stoical in character, not in the sense that we have seen Vico give that term. Bentham, in Mill's words, would judge "a proposition to be true or false as it accorded or not with the result of his own inquiries."[10] Bentham would not inquire into either the meaning that the false proposition had for those who believed it or the historical reasons why the proposition had had value for those who held it. In a word, Bentham lacked the historical sense that would have brought him to investigate and judge the developed specific forms of human thought and action embedded in commonplaces that analytic method might (simply and perhaps destructively) expose as "false." Putting it this way lets us see an inheritance that troubled Mill whose thinking increasingly reflected the more Vichian or Coleridgean curiosity about the workings of mind, the reasons for culture, and the value of topoi — in addition to the severity of their rational truth or falsity. In fact, if we accept Isaiah Berlin's reading of *On Liberty* as a record of how far Mill had traveled from Bentham, we can see that Mill had come to a very new and important position, one that qualifies even Edward Said's association of Mill with Utilitarianism's imperial functions.

In his essay, "Secular Criticism," Said noted that while Mill's liberalism did not bring him to an anti-imperialist position, his work did lead radicals in England and nationalists in India to draw the universal conclusions of his thinking.[11] Said was quoting the work of Eric Stokes, *The English Utilitarians and India*,[12] on a point of historical transmission not unlike that C.L.R. James discussed in *The Black Jacobins*, tracing the influence of the French Revolution's ideals of liberty as one of many strands motivating the Haitian slave revolt against France. Said has described this sort of process in an influential essay, "Traveling Theory,"[13] to which I would like to add a small point drawn from both Mill and Vico.

The Vichian point is familiar from our earlier discussion of commonplaces. Whereas Vico finds Aristotle's categorization of different forms of reason compelling evidence for training in commonplaces, Mill discusses the formation of truth as the creation of commonplaces that must submit, nonetheless, to criticism. Mill wants his readers to understand that the cliché, truth will out, is false. It is false not only in the conventional sense, as a commonplace and error, but as a truth of what dialectical historical reason is. Broadly, Hegel's writings on the relations between reason and history seemed to assure reason's emergence as the truth of history. The early twentieth century saw an intense debate among Marxists and other dialectical thinkers on the left about the relation between human agency — will or intentionality — and the force of history or historical necessity. Mill believed that truth struggled to emerge, more often tamped down by the power of those who profited from consciously held error or unconscious doxologies. Only because of human efforts to criticize, experiment, learn, and teach do truths gain footing, normally through repetition and in the form of commonplaces. Mill's simplest example concerns the emergence of Christian reformation, the impulse of which the combination of Roman Church and European sovereigns repeatedly repressed until in changed — Mill would say more enlightened and freer — circumstances popular judgment and experience provided the medium for its emergence. In other words, Mill provides a historicist's account of the convergence and divergence of truth and commonplace. In Mill, we can find both an account of truth's struggle against error, and also an account of error's alignment with the crudest as well as subtlest forms of power operating upon not only opinion, but upon the body and so upon human subjectivities:

> It is a piece of idle sentimentality that truth, merely as truth, has any inherent power denied to error of prevailing against the dungeon and the stake. . . . The real advantage which truth has consists in this, that when an opinion is true, it may be extinguished once, twice, or many times, and in the course of ages, there will generally be found persons to rediscover it, until some one of its reappearances falls on a time when from favorable circumstances it escapes persecution until it has made such head as to withstand all subsequent attempts to suppress it. (34)

Truth does not so much "travel," as humans "rediscover" it, several times, in different places, and when fortunately placed, it takes hold. Such was the case, for example, with Mill's own thinking about individualism and liberty, which, as we have seen, despite his colonialism, had a liberatory effect upon English radicals and Indian nationalists, alike. A.P. Thornton's historical study of British anti-imperialists records this effect. Mill's own thinking undermined the administrative plans he and other imperialists made to remove politics from "local administration" "by allowing the Bengali *babu* to discuss his own schools and his own drains." As Thornton's analysis shows, these British colonial liberals had a poor knowledge of real historical differences — despite their historicism — and no knowledge at all of Indian resistance. Most important, they had no knowledge of the effects of their universalizing claims: "This was to see the matter in terms somewhat too simple. Minds trained to read, if not always fully to understand, the doctrines of Burke, Mazzini, and Mill, were unlikely long to be content debating issues of schools and drains."[14] Indeed, Thornton takes the epigraph of his book from J.S. Mill, and not entirely, I think, ironically. "Such a thing as the government of one people by another does not and cannot exist."[15] Various forms of subaltern, cultural, and popular studies rightly emphasize the agency if not autonomy of colonized peoples in their struggles against domination. In addition, as I mentioned, Said's critics sometimes object to *Orientalism*'s seeming portrayal of the silent other. I am not suggesting that Mill's or other Europeans' ideas were principle mechanisms for or are adequate explanations of the initiation of postcolonial struggles, although especially in the case of nationalist leaderships educated by colonial masters, the question of influence is complicated but clear. Rather I want to draw attention to the paradoxical value of Mill's thinking about and practice of negative criticism especially as it transcends the limits of his own imperialist mind and prejudice. Further, I want to make clear that Mill's text offers an account of how truths emerge within and as commonplaces and for that historical reason demand, for their own survival, openness to criticism of a kind that challenges them. I stress that they must be open to criticism but not tolerant of anti-liberal politics or thinking that would obviate the truth by solidifying commonplaces away from criticism. In fact, as with Vico, the commonplace has value not as a permanent residence of truth but in its status as something other than the alluring misalliances of apodeisis. On this, Mill is quite clear and critics should internalize this insight as their own:

> The beliefs which we have most warrant for have no safeguard to rest on but a standing invitation to the whole world to prove them unfounded. If the challenge is not accepted, or is accepted and the attempt fails, we are far enough from certainty still, but we have done the best that the existing state of human reason admits of; we have neglected nothing that could give the truth a chance of reaching us; if the lists are kept open, we may hope that, if there be a better truth, it will be found when the human mind is capable of receiving it; and in the meantime we may rely on having attained such approach to truth as is possible in our own day. This is the amount of certainty attainable by a fallible being, and this the sole way of attaining it. (26)

Neoconservatives[16] and fundamentalists alike polemicize against such a complex position, sometimes calling it relativistic and a cause of anomie, other times calling it blasphemy in the face of divine truth, which is permanent, written, and knowable in community. Like the Calvinist who degrades the capacities and values of human will and then does nothing to educate or enhance them, so these polemicists fear and resist an anthropology that allows the human to correct, to learn, to enhance, and, in Vico's terms, complete the gaps in its own culture. They also fear the work humans do upon themselves in social experiment, aesthetic play, and scientific invention — one clear explanation of fundamentalist opposition to stem cell research and evolutionary theory. Criticism has both the negative effects Mill desires — to reveal error, injustice, and intolerance that threaten liberty and human futures — but it also has creative effects, operating upon the human subject who performs it, whom it informs, who figures itself in critical practice. Thus, criticism like all forms of active human will threatens organized religious orthodoxy, political authoritarianism, and social conformism.

Criticism has a double relation to the social conditions for its formation. Its existence depends in part on a social order that accepts the value of active, independent, autonomous judgment as a parry to authority and repression, as a guarantor that the human can evolve historically within its own field of determination, and as a guide to friends' experiments. Of Mill, Berlin writes that it was "his passionate belief that men are made human by their capacity for choice — choice in evil and good equally" (237). Yet, choice must always have its priority in, be belated in relation to the conditions that promote its existence because, seemingly paradoxically, without criticism's judgments the educational and playful improvisatory possibilities that enhance its emergence would themselves have less legitimacy, less reason or means to exist. Of course, fundamentally, these exist as forms and as results or, if you prefer, as embodiments of what we call poetics. Criticism is not only a special form of poesis but as it were, its armature, the device and custom that speaks up for poesis, resists threats to its ambitions, and fortifies it against natural, residual, and modern forms of inertia. Criticism is what we see in Edward Said's lucid description of Mill's work and its place in a cultural system of empire.

Right after first insisting that Mill, in *On Liberty*, disallowed freedom to Indians because they are "civilizationally inferior," Said eloquently articulates his general understanding of the interlacings of texts, culture, and power and so affiliates himself with Mill, whose own "negative criticism" proceeds on similar assumptions, in similar ways, albeit within the blindness of his own Orientalism. "In fine," Said asks, "how can we treat the cultural, historical phenomenon of Orientalism as a kind of *willed human work* — not of mere unconditioned ratiocination — in all its historical complexity, detail, and worth without at the same time losing sight of the alliance between cultural work, political tendencies, the state, and the specific realities of domination?" (15). Said emphasizes that criticism's subject matter is historical culture. In this, he follows Vico and Auerbach and is not far from Mill's analyses of Calvinist societies and concepts (68). Most important, though, in each of these cases, the critic treats culture as "willed human work," that is, criticism approaches its materials as a nexus resulting from human agency, situatedness, and willful production. Texts, for example, as work or as "works," not only are the embodied result of agency, the complexity of which requires historical analysis, but are products of will, of intent, of power that continues, vector-like, throughout space and time, to elaborate themselves throughout and as historical culture. By this logic and in fact, criticism is itself an act of will, an instance of work that, as Mill taught, stands ready to defend and enact the human capacity to resist its own arrest.

Said's view of critical obligation rests on an anthropological sense of the historical human of a kind that, I argue, shares a family resemblance, is deeply affiliated with Mill's sense of the human and of historical humanity's capacities to elaborate itself culturally and politically, eudaimonistically — that is, toward its own perfection. Said's heirs sometimes accuse him of both Eurocentrism and elitism for making Euro-American materials the center of his critique — thereby repeating Orientalism's silencing of the other — and for adopting the achievements of European artistic masterpieces as a defining measure of human cultural value and political purpose. In other words, Said greatly admires Andalusian culture during the Caliphate of Córdoba not only for the fact of its relatively tolerant and highly creative diversity, for the richness of cultural life woven from Islam, Judaism, and Christianity — and its heritage from Normandy across the Mediterranean. He celebrates also the elaborated cultural achievements of a time and place that enabled both great art and a social world that valued, encouraged, and produced it as a measure of its own ambitions. Criticism judges the complex interplay of art and the extended cultural practices of state and society according to a measure set by the highest achievements in human fields of poesis.

People err in calling this elitism. In its combination of great achievements in politics, art, and social life such historical moments are not merely measures of humans' occasional greatness but as such testimony to possibilities. It is of the essence that humanistic scholarship should be historically comparative so that no particular epoch or civil arrangement comes to seem natural or complete, without strengths and weaknesses. This is the great lesson of Vico's comparison of the advantages and disadvantages of ancient and modern study methods. Especially in times of war and violence against entire populations and alternative modes of life and thought, criticism must not only reevaluate the vested values of contemporary production but also compare them to others, the records of which scholarship can read and criticism must judge. Such a view is not only modern, as it were, "after" Vico. It is also a very traditional position, available in the West since Aristotle (*Nicomachaean Ethics*) and among Arab and Persian commentators on his work, especially Ibn Rushd, called Averroes in Europe. It takes on new meaning with Western modernity's discovery and creation of eudaimonia as a historical capacity of the human, as a matter of reason and will producing culture as the elaborated product of humanity's emergence.

As far as I can tell, analytic philosophers understand liberalism and perfectionism to be cancelling opposites. That is, they argue that liberals like Mill cannot simultaneously hold perfectionist aspirations for the human. If we take John Rawls as an authoritative voice among liberal political philosophers, then this claim appears simple. As one of his commentators explains, "Rawls sees perfectionism as the enemy of the liberty and autonomy that are the birthright of all individuals in a just and liberal society." In this tradition, "'perfectionism' tends to convey the idea that the best life for humans is the most perfect they can live, the kind of life that is the best expression of their nature."[17] "All individuals" cannot possibly achieve the "best life for humans" imagined in these terms; as a result, what is good for each person according to her own lights and experience is degraded as a departure from "the best." As another commentator explains about this tradition, it aims "at purifying liberal justice of any appeal to perfectionist ideals so as to avoid ranking some one as superior to the others."[18]

I feel generous in saying that these philosophers make a typically Cartesian error, Cartesian in that Vichian sense we discussed earlier. Nevertheless, we must hammer home the point that criticism has the advantage in its historicism and should not yield to a romance with philosophy's supposedly higher status. Philosophers insist that reason does not allow liberalism to be perfectionist because perfectionist ethics are as Rawls and others maintain anti-democratic and elitist. Reading Mill in such terms, following such methods, makes it impossible to understand the historical nature of his claims for human potentiality. For example, Mill concedes that during periods of authoritarian and dogmatic domination great individual minds and artists can rise to heights and achieve great things. Such situations dissatisfy Mill. His passion is for a much more inclusive standard, one that does not sacrifice the majority or, indeed, the minority — even if a minority of one — to the benefit of an elite, of genius, or unique accomplishment. While analytic philosophers debate seemingly endlessly the refinements necessary to adjust the relations between liberalism and ideas of human perfection, concluding that the two are contradictory, Mill insists on socio-cultural transformations accomplished over time, in education and politics that would so alter the historical circumstances as to make his ambitions possible. In a properly conceived polity, there should be, would be, no choice between the achievement of the one and the accomplishments of the many. The analyst's approach, so thoroughly ahistorical, misses the fact that differing realities alter the terms of conceptualization. Mill admits "There have been, and may again be, great individual thinkers, in a general atmosphere of mental slavery." Despite, for example, the success of a Solzhenitsyn in the Gulag, of a Gramsci in a Fascist prison, or of a Hu Feng in Maoist internment, Mill urges his readers to understand the greater civilizational value in another mode of human life and to internalize the idea as their own ideal:

> But there never has been, nor ever will be, in that atmosphere an intellectually active people. Where any people has made a temporary approach to such a character, it has been because the dread of heterodox speculation was for a time suspended. Where there is a tacit convention that principles are not to be disputed, where the discussion of the greatest questions which can occupy humanity is considered to be closed, we cannot hope to find that generally high scale of mental activity which has made some periods of history so remarkable. Never when controversy avoided the subjects which are large and important enough to kindle enthusiasm was the mind of the people stirred up from its foundations, and the impulse given which raised even persons of the most ordinary intellect to something of the dignity of thinking beings. (39)

Recall Mill's context and ours, in Hong Kong, in the People's Republic, or in the United States — the market's autonomy and efficiency is an unquestioned if not quite unquestionable principle. As a result, at least in the United States, individuals and groups cannot and do not experiment easily with forms of life or thought that market principles do not allow or endorse. In the United States, for example, a combination of market principles and supposed Christian orthodoxy obstruct homosexual lives and the social experiments and intellectual probings they induce. The highest-ranking general in the United States Army told a Chicago newspaper "that he believed homosexual conduct was immoral and akin to adultery." The next day, he announced "his support for current Pentagon policy that prohibits openly gay people from serving in the armed forces."[19] As we expect in a pluralistic society, supporters of gay rights and other advocates of human rights strongly objected to the general's remarks and actions. Mill would not consider this a healthy situation, despite the position some American liberals might take in defense of free speech rights in the United States. Mill would notice that the general did not lose his job; he would notice that many others, often in key social positions, defended the general's statements, and, indeed, polemicized against free speech advocates, not merely disagreeing with their arguments, but with their very right to criticize authority and institutionalized orthodoxies. In sum, this drama does not represent what Mill imagines a healthy society should be. It does not accept that it should correct itself, that debate and discussion matter — only elements of the society believe that — and those in authority seem to believe it least of all.

In such situations, while individual minds might flourish and groups of individuals might progress, the social whole cannot, precisely because the health of the social whole, which depends on experiment, discussion, and criticism, is not a goal, not an ambition of a power arrangement that would deracinate all forms of human subjectivity different from or in opposition to its own. In a society that worked to enable the highest possible general level of human activity and thought, errors would occur; powers would solidify; but corrigibility would function as a critical ideal, internalized, so to speak, in consciousness and institutions. Moreover, the analytic philosopher who cannot grasp — no matter how careful the conceptual and terminological distinctions — how rhetorically effective liberal topoi might serve human perfection imagines a different world than Mill and a different role for mind and human judgment. Mill imagines a world in which the ideal of a "high scale of mental activity" is the dominant concrete socio-political ambition, a possibility that rests on a different historical conception of the human, one in which there is no reason to believe that what analysis assumes and suggests — what is now the case will always be *per secula seculorum.* Something, yet, unites the analysts and the opponents of free speech. It is certainly not a common commitment to forms of authoritarianism. In their common ahistoricism, however, they embody what Mill considers the greatest threat to freedom and historicality: "in maintaining this principle, the greatest difficulty to be encountered does not lie in the appreciation of means toward an acknowledged end, but in the indifference of persons in general to the end itself" (63).

On Liberty's passion comes from Mill's strong conviction that to be itself the human must, individually and civilizationally, struggle to reach its own perfect state, that is, the highest state possible that its natural and intellectual resources allow. I agree with Berlin that *On Liberty* is not primarily a Utilitarian essay, but I take seriously Mill's early statement that all human ethics must be "grounded on the permanent interests of man as a progressive being" (15). There is a rich ambiguity here and once the second possibility occurs to the mind, it seems the more interesting. First, man has permanent interests and they are in his fate as a progressive being. Second, insofar as man is a "progressive being," which is a matter of history as much if not more than a matter of nature, then ethics rest on interests that are permanent for the human as progressive. If and when man is not "man as a progressive being," then the ethics that Mill goes on to describe — including individualism, freedom of choice, speech, action — lose their ground and indeed their status as important ethical questions. In other words, Mill's interest is in the historical being and concept, "man as a progressive being."

The second possibility rather than the first not only separates Mill from Bentham but also makes his ethics and his critical thinking more interesting. We can see the great importance Mill gives to incompletion, to temporal change, to the openness of possibility embodied not only in the humility that recognizes the persistence of error but also the variety of human experience and its function as an essential basis for human corrigibility. Of course, experience is not sufficient; corrigibility is possible because the human mind is such a thing as to learn by correction — an emergent ability that enhances human possibilities.[20] On a basis that is itself the result of human action, experience, with free discussion and free experiments in life practice, affords the vision of individuals, the species, and of civilization as perfectible. As utopian as that word sounds in the ear of any critic, we know that Mill meant for us to understand perfectibility as at any and all times an ideal and as potential limited by time and history. In fact, criticism is the defining mark of historical circumstantiality and the enemy of all systems of thought and politics that would arrest human change within structures of self-assured or highly anxious authority. Criticism reflects the confidence of the human, of mind, and of society in the value of its own discussions, judgments, and experiences, despite or indeed in the face of all these historical transformations it has brought about and which it must understand — no matter if these fall in the realm of politics, language, or intellect.

In each period of human history, whatever is "perfect" is always, as it were, over the horizon, a motive, perhaps a vision or prospect, but certainly distanced. Mill knows that diversity of opinion is an evolutionary advantage to the historically human that must continue, "until mankind shall have entered the stage of intellectual advancement which at present seems at an incalculable distance" (51). No person can acquire wisdom or influence, a reputation for right judgment, without passing through such formative processes as might create trust. What happens to the individual, would best happen to societies, to the species:

> In the case of any person whose judgment is really deserving of confidence, how has it become so? Because he has kept his mind open to criticism of his opinions and conduct. Because it has been his practice to listen to all that could be said against him; to profit by as much of it as was just, and expound to himself, and upon occasion to others, the fallacy of what was fallacious. Because he has felt, that the only way in which a human being can make some approach to knowing the whole of a subject, is by hearing what can be said about it by persons of every variety of opinion, and studying all modes in which it can be looked at by every character of mind. No wise man ever acquired his

wisdom in any mode but this; nor is it in the nature of human intellect to become wise in any other manner. The steady habit of correcting and completing his own opinion by collating it with those of others, so far from causing doubt and hesitation in carrying it into practice, is the only stable foundation for a just reliance on it. (24)

Judgment, confidence, wisdom, intellect, debate, openness — qualities once thought essential to all critical practice but now sometimes set aside by mere technical or professional expertise. It is a painful sign of imperialism's power that these notions served empire and race divisions, but the ideal of listening, as far as it applies, for example, to state intellectuals' obligations to hear the others they intend to isolate or combat should hold much greater sway. Isaiah Berlin, in 1959, during the Cold War, after the horrors of British violence in Kenya, at the height of tortuous violence in the Algerian War of Independence lamented that Mill's principles had not yet become "undisputed assumptions of a civilized outlook" (230). Violence because of certainty, of ignorant confidence, as censorship of criticism, complexity, and truth — this nexus represents a civilization that would destroy the historically human, which Mill, like Vico, Auerbach, and others, sees as the as yet best achievement of the species, the form that promises futures and that demands respect for learning, thinking, and correction. Isaiah Berlin wanted his audience to know that Mill understood the links among crude violence, the hidden because agreed upon forms of political and social conformity, and the potentiality that the human created for itself through struggle into a certain form of modernity:

> What he hated and feared was narrowness, uniformity, the crippling effects of persecution, the crushing of individuals by the weight of authority or of custom or of public opinion; he set himself against the worship of order or tidiness, or even peace, if they were bought at the price of obliterating the variety and color of untamed human beings with unextinguished passions and untrammeled imaginations. (221)

It is astonishing, of course, that Berlin's last clause is true of an imperialist, but within this conundrum, Mill enhanced the comparative historicist's devotion to the variety and creativity of the human while limiting its consequences to Europeans. Mill defended what has become within Western modernity a common trope, one that extends at least from Vico to Auerbach and Said, one that laments modernity's destruction of heterogeneity, its creation of powers that violently enforce a monochromatic world of mind and social life. We can find similarities between Berlin's expression of his anxiety on Mill's part and that of Berlin's contemporary, Hannah Arendt, who differently but with similar passion worried the emergence of American consumerism and Americanized culture as a forced leveling of differences among all peoples. Of course, what I call Mill's conundrum reinforced another quite horrible effect, namely, the sort of identity politics, the practices of differentiation that ironically enable the violence that Mill lamented. Mill's persistent exclusion of the Chinese and Indians from the domain of liberal life, of individual privilege, of political freedom and self-determination added to an imperial science of fundamental difference. He helped authorize those who arrogated liberal privileges to themselves the right to not only rule and dominate but also when felt necessary, to wage war upon the illiberal or not yet liberal "other."[21] In that paradox, the power of Western modernity, always tempted as Vico showed, to imperial practice, generated violence that in the name of wild diversity and experiment warred against and summoned violence from those whose "otherness" is so radical as to be outside the range not only of orthodoxy, but of heterodoxy, itself. In essence, Mill's liberalism embodied and enhanced the modern Western conflict between violence and poesis, an awkward tangle that haunts a great deal of liberalism until today. If we unwind the humanistic historicism from within Mill, as I have been attempting to do, we can see how essential criticism is to liberalism. It is liberalism's key value and, as such, we should recall its power now, in an era when nothing more pleases the openly violent and hateful than the destruction of those liberal realities that hedge them in. I refer, of course, to such events as the Bush administration's assault on the rule of law, on free speech and privacy, and on the claims of reality among those it derogates as "reality-based."

> The [President's] aide said that guys like me were "in what we call the reality-based community," which he defined as people who "believe that solutions emerge from your judicious study of discernible reality." I nodded and murmured something about enlightenment principles and empiricism. He cut me off. "That's not the way the world really works anymore," he continued. "We're an empire now, and when we act, we create our own reality. And while you're studying that reality — judiciously, as you will — we'll act again, creating other new realities, which you can study too, and that's how things will sort out. We're history's actors . . . and you, all of you, will be left to just study what we do."[22]

The Baconians among us find it horribly easy to laugh at such arrogant ignorance, to say that knowing history and culture, for example, might prevent such bungling as the Iraq War. Knowledge, even total or encyclopedic knowledge, is no alternative; after all, the nineteenth-century imperialists produced enormous bodies of scientific knowledge about subject populations — or so they thought — and that helped little in maintaining imperial control. Moreover, knowledge requires thinking and what this arrogant American represents is the absence of thinking and the substitution for it of technological power, will, and poesis corrupted by detachment from reality and criticism.

Historical humanism, especially formed in literature, has, as we have already seen, both a creative effect and a moral political responsibility to the real — neither of which this destructive fetishizing of power displays. Mill's contradictory position, his imperial embrace of universal liberty sheltered by the West but denied to the rest, suffered from a similar detachment of reality. *On Liberty* not only has no sublimity to its vision of universal freedom — that would have required an impossible radicalism — but it also has no contact with the quotidian elements of social reality that would link the human to life in the world, or imbue human life with the complex tangibility of extension, objects, and time.

Despite these limits, Mill left criticism with a legacy of two important tools, negative criticism, and a portrait of human finitude — our subjects for the next time.

5
John Stuart Mill and the Limits of Self-Making

I n 1962, the Nobel Prize laureate and American novelist, Saul Bellow wrote:

> In what we call the novel of sensibility the intent of the writer is to pull
> us into an all-sufficient consciousness which he, the writer, governs
> absolutely. In the realistic novel today the writer is satisfied with an art
> of externals. Either he assumes that by describing a man's shoes he has
> told us all that we need to know about his soul, or he is more interested
> in the shoes than in the soul.[1]

In this little essay Bellow analyzes those readers and cultural habits, especially
in the United States, that blur the distinction between art and knowledge. He
mocks the reader who decides on a work's merit not by affective, moral, or
aesthetic response, but by locating the work in some positive index of knowledge,
normally the index of accuracy or information. So, Bellow laments the editors
who "fact check," knowing readers will judge a novel's value by how accurately
the urban writer portrays intersections and building heights. He criticizes the
performance and entertainment industries for coddling viewers and audiences
with measures of exactness, of familiarity, of normal expectations. He warns
of the dire social and intellectual consequences inherent in an art world that
assumes it must neither discomfit, nor surprise, nor educate its audience, its
readership, or its population.

Scholars and public opinion rightly think of Bellow as a realistic novelist.
Bellow claims his pedigree from the great nineteenth-century European
tradition, which differed from his contemporary American emphasis on facts
and knowledge alone: "The realistic method made it possible to write with
seriousness and dignity about the ordinary, common situations of life. In Balzac,
Flaubert, and the great Russian masters the realistic externals were intended
to lead inward. I suppose one might say that now the two elements, the

inward and the external, have come apart." Readers of modern literature are accustomed to Bellow's pleas for an integrated art, one that achieves relations between consciousness and externality to maintain the strong links essential to historicism among human thought, work, and material world. Of course, as we have already seen in discussing Erich Auerbach, even European intellectuals feared the same dissociation that worries Bellow. In the post-war era, Bellow's reflexive worry that American difference from Europe will degrade humanistic art's potential for sustaining the integral reality of man and world belongs to the same set of concerns as those voiced not only by Auerbach but by Hannah Arendt.[2] If Americanism is, as Bellow fears, a threat to historical humanism, then we are back on familiar ground with new names, that is, we have returned to the analysis that Vico worked out in contrasting tendencies within modernity itself. In his essay, America is the alternative to aesthetic success in sustaining the completion of human subjectivity intertwined with a world and its objects. Bellow is very near despair over the same question Auerbach posed in regards to Woolf and the other consciousness-novelists of classical modernity. Rather than fearing a pseudo-Joycean emphasis upon self-sufficient consciousness, the fictional equivalent of naïve idealism, Bellow fears the complacency of information as a substitute for the demanding task of creating art and responding to it in ways that allow it to do its work in forming integrated human subjects. It results in an unbalanced culture he indicts for worse than indifference:

> The American desire for the real has created a journalistic sort of novel which has a *thing* excitement, a glamour of *process;* it specializes in information. It resembles the naturalistic novel of Zola and the social novel of Dreiser, but is without the theoretical interests of the first and is unlike the second in that it has no concern with justice and no view of fate. It merely satisfies the readers' demand for knowledge. From this standpoint it may sometimes be called an improving or moral sort of book. However, it seldom has much independent human content, and it is more akin to popularized science or history than to the fiction of Balzac or Chekhov. It is not actively challenged by the "novel of sensibility."

Bellow's essay is unsatisfying, however, because the proper human relations between consciousness and the extended world of life do not result from a struggle between Americanism and sensibility. That America has no novel of sensibility seems patently false, if we remember the work of Henry James and his heirs, although Bellow thinks little of them. (Needless to say, "sensibility" does not exhaust the richness of James's formal art.) Nevertheless, a healthy culture does not result from internecine Manichean struggles and critics who believe so soon become unhelpful partisans. More to the point, Bellow wants to solve a problem that inheres in modernity, with the question now posed in terms of its development into late forms of constant innovation that threaten by consumerism and indexicalism literary culture's creation of integrated historical human subjects.

Bellow's concern for a realism that art and audience alike respect and to which they are responsible implies an ethical foundation in the perfectionist goal of liberal individualism that we recognize in Mill, especially in his Tocquevillian moments of anxiety over mass taste and majority authority in democracies. We see his anxiety in the phrase, "independent human content," as if for the great realists from Dante to Woolf there were such hypostatized, almost natural substances. Curiously, for a realist, Bellow, right in so many of his diagnoses of consumerist and indexicalist culture, is wrong in his literary history and theory of literature's proper role. He has a weak and anxious response to modernity's traps; in his legacy, the creative historical role of literature and the persistent, perhaps evolutionary capacity for poesis disappears into a bitter resentment at loss. Auerbach's Woolf, if we draw a comparison, is a writer of great strength whose art creates forms appropriate to needful times that demand transformations of technique rather than retrospective lament of turns away from inherited forms that are no longer adequate to the writer's responsibility to the real. In short, Bellow does not think through the lesson of error. Attitudinizing is not judgment or history — and it is not literature at its best.

Consider by contrast the summary point Michael Wood, who has also — as we shall see — written appreciatively about William Empson, makes about the novels of Richard Powers. In especially Powers's late novels, Wood finds the proper and difficult achievement of literature's proper poetic responsibility to the real. Powers's art is far beyond moralistic fictions that compensate for what to a lesser poet seems the abnormal and easily correctable dissociation of subjectivity. "The point," Wood writes, "is not the seepage of fiction into what used to be real life, but the difficulty of finding fictions that engage with what isn't fiction; and of knowing when the fictions . . . are going to help us or delude us."[3] What for Bellow is and can be made "correct" depends not on art but coercion; art, poetry, and criticism are the domains of error, the entanglements of which with real life, as with Woolf's brown stocking, create and enhance the life of humans and of the human in history, in place, and in its own efforts to emerge.

John Stuart Mill makes error an essential concern in *On Liberty*, where he thinks error in terms of both human finitude and human historicality. As we all know, nineteenth-century Western European literary and critical cultures record consistent thinking about what we now call "self-making," that is, analyses that take human formation as aesthesis, as the result of aesthetic sensibility at work in judging and creating one's own ethos and style. By the end of the century, especially in the writings of Walter Pater, this interest culminated in an alliance between individual self-creation, performance and the self, and the psychological structures that enable and restrain the sensibilities that guide self-creation. Within this complex archive, Mill has a small but anticipatory place. His essay on Coleridge, for example, has more in common with Pater's later "portraits" and "studies" than with what we think of now as critical articles. More important, for our purposes, Mill's pages on Marcus Aurelius work out the seductive dangers associated with not only knowledge and moral responsibility but also the romance of self-making. Although Mill's Emperor might be a hero in a novel of sensibility, as Bellow describes it, his complex and rich inwardness does nothing to protect him and others from tragic decisions. Mill tells a story of failure and error on a scale that makes trivial-seeming most aesthetic narratives of personal self-formation, taken as matters of style or psychological universalism. The stories of Des Esseintes or Axel are of no interest in comparison to the consequential story of Marcus Aurelius's errant self-regard. In an important way, Mill's comments push toward later moments in Nietzsche and Foucault, and should finally set aside philosophical "demonstrations" that "perfectionism" cannot function as an historical or ethical terrain for thinking the human or its futures.

Criticism has everything to do with will. Modern Anglo-American critics knew this and worked to establish the fact as justification for specific methods of reading and pedagogy. Certainly, they are uneven in their results and not always admirable in their intentions.[4] As far as criticism is an agency of poesis and the weapon defending the human from threats within and without, we cannot discuss it without understanding error's place within the critical will. Now, this topic is endless; speculation would carry us very far and the history of criticism, from Plato at least, would absorb us in the entire archive of Western literary and critical work. Nonetheless, each critic must confront it as a danger to and of the critic's calling. Paul de Man once famously wrote that "Literature exists at the same time in the modes of error and truth; it both betrays and obeys its own mode of being." Until recently, this insight had been a truism of literary criticism, but were there time I think we could demonstrate that it is false in any meaningful way. That is, I think we could demonstrate that no matter how we construe the word, "betray," literature is the one way of being that cannot commit error, knowing always and "betraying" always its own escape from the epistemological fields of error and truth.

Criticism, no doubt a relative of literature, cannot be free of error as literature can.[5] Criticism's enactment of the will and its entanglements with truth and rhetoric in persuasion, in the speed of the commonplace, makes it available for correction and for horrible as well as creative direct effects. Mill portrays Marcus Aurelius because the Emperor impressed him and his willful critical errors moved Mill to a nearly tragic pathos. He introduces Marcus Aurelius in the context of discussing how the best people can and do make the most egregious and violent errors. He starts this section of *On Liberty* with stories of unjust deaths of great men, and he comes quickly to the Christian story of atonement. Rather than condemn Christ's murderers for ignorance, hypocrisy, and blasphemy, however, he reminds us that they were better men than most:

> Men did not merely mistake their benefactor, they mistook him for the exact contrary of what he was and treated him as that prodigy of impiety which they themselves are now held to be for their treatment of him. The feelings with which mankind now regard these lamentable transactions . . . render them extremely unjust in their judgement of the unhappy actors. These were, to all appearances, not bad men — not worse than men commonly are, but rather the contrary; men who possessed in a full, or somewhat more than a full measure, the religious, moral, and patriotic feelings of their time and people: the very kind of men who, in all times, our own included, have every chance of passing through life blameless and respected. (30)

In the final lecture, I will resume Mill's line of thought here with a discussion of William Empson's daring reading of George Herbert. First, let me set aside a normal line of objection to Mill's position. Of course, his provocative remarks seem to be of a kind that merely justify any given status quo, a result that liberalism's critics claim it usually produces. The best men could have done nothing more; it is unjust to judge them harshly. Gestures of that form legitimate all sorts of horrors. More radically, Mill's critics admit, however, he works out a sort of critical situationalism, one that serves not to justify any given social norm, especially not the one that led to Christ's crucifixion. Rather, his thinking is more daring; ultimately, he is not so much interested in the ordinarily good men of the kind who killed Christ. His target is much more interesting. He aims to show how profoundly dangerous are the most self-assured, well-formed, highly educated, and normative intellectuals and populations. They lack humility, self-criticism, and awareness that their own finitude puts them in need of those who appear to them to be heretical. Without those qualities, power leads to violence of the most torturous and murderous kind. In this context, Mill offers Marcus Aurelius as the best (or most sad) example of a refined self-created wise persona, a human subject without historicality or humility, that in its willed actions gives human finitude the seemingly inescapable face of extreme violence and deracination. In addition, his self-confident hatred of the heretics brought him into ironic union with the Roman multitude — an egregious failure of insightful will.

"Let us add one more example," Mill says, to the gallery of persecution; "the most striking of all, if the impressiveness of an error is measured by the wisdom and virtue of him who falls into it." Neither Lear, nor Hamlet, nor Othello have wisdom and virtue in Mill's sense; perhaps Oedipus is a closer approximation to the tragically flawed Marcus Aurelius, especially in a common desire to save their cities with tactics that rest equally on their formidable sense of responsibility and confidence in their own judgments. Yet, Marcus Aurelius, unlike Oedipus, has a choice to allow the openly heretical to function as the critical other to his own intelligence. Sophocles gives Oedipus a choice that becomes apparent only after disaster. History, however, presents Marcus Aurelius with precisely the challenge of emergence that Vico notes imperialists and their intellectuals always refuse, taking recourse to violence to assure order.

Before we follow Mill into his critical reading of Marcus Aurelius, note that he accuses the Emperor philosopher of a different fault than he does the persecutors of Christ. Those merely committed a mistake, a failure of recognition. They misread the object of their interest and they misread their situation. They mistook fact and circumstance. Marcus Aurelius, however, more sadly and fatally erred, that is, he lost his way, he wandered and, in Mill's subtle echo of the story of Thales and the well, "falls into [error]."

Marcus Aurelius is not only a Roman Emperor, but also a Stoic philosopher of standing whose writings Mill greatly admired, once having compared his *Meditations* to the "Sermon on the Mount" in Matthew's Gospel. In *On Liberty*, Mill's portrait contrasts him with Christ's murderers in kind, not just degree. He is not the most "striking example" of misreading, of mis-taking, or misprision, but of Mill's profound point that error is ubiquitous and requires of all absolute openness to criticism and alternatives.

At first sight, the Jewish High Priest and Roman Emperor commonly persecute Christ and Christians. Each acts from a sense of responsibility, the first a better-than-common person, the second, a well-positioned genius. It is significant that Mill tells us nothing of the High Priest's formation but stresses Marcus Aurelius's intellectual self-formation. The High Priest is notably "sincere" rather than cynical and corrupt; and he acted, Mill adds, as most conforming Christians in England in the nineteenth century would act if they felt so threatened and outraged.

Marcus Aurelius, by contrast, is in no way common. Unlike the High Priest or conformist, he opts for "indulgence" and "tenderness" rather than strictness and routine. He has courage and the confidence to pioneer in thought and life. And yet, he ordered the persecution and torture of Christians, enacting barbarities of a kind that became too common in the late Roman Empire and then again later in the Roman and Spanish Inquisitions, and finally in modern forms of state torture and genocide.

Mill has considerable insight into the limits of the idea of aesthetic self-fashioning that became such a common nineteenth- and indeed twentieth-century literary and critical trope after Schiller and on to recent developments in performance and gender studies. At the same time, his insight's limits are severe and they result mostly from his inability or unwillingness, his seeming failure to realize the value of close philological examination of Marcus Aurelius's life and work. Mill has the Stoic Emperor right as a case, but his abstraction limits our understanding of Marcus Aurelius and the complexities of thinking, culture, law, and language involved in the case. For Mill, what matters is that the most refined mind at the pinnacle of human achievement committed murderous errors that afflicted Western history for centuries.

At first, Marcus appears to be the sublime human subject capable of all that humanity might achieve. He has about him complexity, knowledge, sensitivity, highly refined sensibility, and generosity. He makes him seem representative of modernity's ideals of the aesthetic sensibility, of the self-fashioned artist that fulfills human potentiality. Despite all his qualities of mind and character, of education and judgment, he could not transcend human finitude's limitations of mind:

> Placed at the summit of all the previous attainments of humanity, with an open, unfettered intellect, and a character which led him of himself to embody in his moral writings the Christian ideal, he yet failed to see that Christianity was to be a good and not an evil to the world, with his duties to which he was so deeply penetrated.

Should we have expected more from Marcus Aurelius than from the High Priest of Jerusalem? There is a subtle difference between the latter's mistaking of Christ and the former's failure to see. Marcus Aurelius's failure is oddly futural: he could not see that the new religion "was to be a good." He lacked the sort of anticipatory intelligence that the modern historical thinker, Mill, makes a criterion of moral and political judgment. The Emperor's failure to see exemplifies a recurrent motif in Mill's explication of tragic failure:

> Existing society he knew to be in a deplorable state. But such as it was, he saw, or thought he saw, that it was held together, and prevented from being worse, by belief and reverence of the received divinities. As a ruler of mankind, he deemed it his duty not to suffer society to fall in pieces; and saw not how, if its existing ties were removed, any others could be formed which could again knit it together. . . . Inasmuch . . . as the theology of Christianity did not appear to him true or of divine origin, inasmuch as this strange history of a crucified God was not credible to him, and a system which purported to rest entirely upon a foundation to him so wholly unbelievable, could not be foreseen by him to be that renovating agency which, after all its abatements, it has in fact proved to be; the gentlest and most amiable of philosophers and rulers, under a solemn sense of duty, authorized the persecution of Christianity. To my mind this is one of the most tragical facts in all history. (31)

Abstractly and after the fact, history has corrected Marcus's judgment: Christianity renovated society for the good. To the critic, there is no interest in ex-post-facto knowledge or judgment. Since Mill does not do the careful philology he should have done to help us understand the Emperor's errancy, we can at best approximate what appeared to Mill's mind to be the flaws that this most accomplished man shows to be typical or insurmountable.

Mill expected this Stoic philosopher to prospect whereas, in fact, those very qualities that Mill identifies as the basis for taking his actions as tragical rather than merely cruel, are not those of a prospector. In Vico's terms, it might seem too harsh to describe Marcus as a pioneer, a sapper, a military figure more concerned with order and occupation than emergence of history. Marcus was merely being responsible to society's need for order. Mill is sympathetic. He does not understand, however, why Marcus's judgment fails. In a word, like most imperial rulers, he cannot and will not tolerate an emergent reordering that might create a new world. Equally important, Marcus is a Stoic and as Mill's language emphasizes, his judgment rests on a habit of truth-testing that cripples his judgment, adding to his imperial intolerance of emergence. Marcus found Christ and Christianity incredible, untrue, and unbelievable. Although this is an odd mixture of negations, in sum they represent that Stoic habit of reducing reason to the uniformity of certainty that Vico lamented destroyed the Republic of Letters and displaced the public good of dialectical reason, the topoi, with a skepticism without reserve. The skeptical and incredulous Emperor chose the order he knew over that he did not; chose the status quo in decline over the conversation of disagreement; and chose the force of pioneering empire over the emergence of new peoples and new orders in time. In short, he chose against history and against humanity's emergent nature.

Recent philosophical commentary suggests limits to Mill's style of liberalism, claiming that liberals of his sort can do no more than dwell in an ironic attitude toward their own judgment that cruelty is the worst of things. Of course, such a critique, even by avowed progressives or anti-fundamentalist postmoderns is, in my opinion, seriously disabled. For the moment, the issue is neither anti-fundamentalism, nor relativism, nor — except partly — a consequential anomie. The issue is the fate of the human's relation to history. Characteristically, the non-historicist practice of these philosophers disallows an understanding of the emergent processes that infuse the human and history into a project that is substantially more ambitious than the wan irony of such "anti-liberals." These philosophers, who hope to "achieve" not only their countries but also their own reputations, secure in their disciplinary walls, are contributing elements to the impoverished societies they claim to regret. Worse, they are political and intellectual cowards who declare inescapable as historical fact the impoverished resentment of their own imaginative abjection.[6]

Marcus has qualities like those Mill gives Bentham in his portrait of Coleridge and like those Vico gives not only to the Stoics but also to the Cartesians and their heirs. We now also recognize them as the qualities modern aestheticism and modern ethics have assigned to the intellectual and consumer classes within the metaphor of "self-making." If there is a question that arises, it is how to make the self — that is again, the question of how human subjectivity forms itself. Moreover, the first part of any answer must be, "historically," or in Vichian terms, poetically and critically.

No matter what Mill thought of Christianity, Marcus is guilty of a secular error, namely, the inability to see the concrete and material realities in which his life, thought, and responsibility rested. In a word, he lacked realism, that ethical responsibility to the real that Vico thought after Dante would be a permanent part of historical civilization's ethos. Stoically, Marcus substituted his analysis of theology and story for study and knowledge; he had abstract method but no knowledge. He analyzed but had no sense of Christians' language, no anthropological sense. He constructed a dichotomy of true/false and us/them.

Within this familiar imperial construct, despite his open mind and his privileged cultural position, he lacked aesthetic competence. If we adopt the classical dichotomy, we would say that Marcus lived in the world of thinkable but immaterial things (*nohta*) rather than perceptible and material things (*aisqhta*).[7] Moreover, he had no idea of what after Dante we call historicism and no political disposition to the end or reorganization of his empire.

Mill would seem to have it that Marcus had sensitivity and sensibility but made an egregious error. Marcus's errancy is not, however, his alone, but that of a type whose violent consequences must be kept in mind if we hope to understand better how to organize human subjectivity, how to value such possibilities, and how to defend the human aim to create itself as an historical object. If there is to be sensibility and sensitivity, they can be neither simple internalized opponents to facts and information nor the sublime achievements of a self-made mind that takes itself as a culmination and eschews the comparative method and ideal of corrigibility. Marcus Aurelius would have benefited from what Mill called "negative critique," that is, the clear and forceful articulation of failure without the obligation to provide an alternative. Mill understood how calling for an alternative silences criticism and allows error to persist rather than exposing it, demanding its defense or justification, requiring its relegitimation or ending in its delegitimation. The mind that accepts the force of negative criticism settles into neither the assured methodological criteria of skepticism nor the imperial ambitions of order. Moreover, it never translates orthodoxy into violence because it starts out accepting the necessary value of heresy for its own health and for the perfection of the human. In the case of Marcus Aurelius, as in more recent cases, rulers might not think to prop up or renew their own crumbling society by reorganizing it around and through violence aimed at its putatively threatening other.

Criticism and error are deeply intertwined, and critics are no more protected from error than any other person is. It is perfectly reasonable to say that ordinary people, even those like the High Priest, who are better than most, are incapable of error, no matter how often they make mistakes. What then does Mill think about error and its relation to criticism?

First, criticism is not and cannot be only a personal, private, or individual act. Second, its benefits depend upon its public status, upon its protected and, indeed, admired and encouraged position within a social order. Third, it is so forceful as to require careful delimitation by correlative values and practices. Chief among these last is humility. If its outcome is not to be disaster or ill consequence, then it must detach itself from forms of power that are instrumental and dangerously different from those of criticism itself.

Marcus Aurelius's errancy is easily theorized but its historicization clarifies how thoroughly misplaced are abstract expectations that criticism might find its home within imperial forms of power and thought. It has become an easy slogan that critics must speak truth to power; Mill certainly embraces that position. *On Liberty* is nothing if not a challenge to several ruling orthodoxies, even if it is far from radical enough in its specific historical analyses. As important, though, are Mill's emphases upon the social factors and the intellectual factors that together guide criticism through the dangers of errancy.

Throughout his essay, Mill gives prominence to the importance of heresy and heretics. His basic position puzzles the reader when it first appears: "those who have been in advance of society . . . preferred endeavoring to alter the feelings of mankind on the particular points on which they were themselves heretical rather than make common cause in defence of freedom with heretics generally" (11). If we keep this remark in mind, we would know that Marcus could only be errant. Moreover, in a way that is odd to at least the commonsense view of liberalism, Mill seems to argue against the primacy of reform, against the calculations that advance a social world incrementally. While there is certainly nothing here approaching Marx's contemporary call for revolutionary change or anything near Marx's theorizing revolution in *The Eighteenth Brumaire*, there is a strong claim that alliance among the heretical is necessary for freedom. Criticism, even in its most simply negative form, cannot, then, defend freedom or protect the capacity for poetry if it localizes itself within a certain area of protest or conversion. While the individual heretic maintains the efficacious truth of heresy in the face of orthodoxy, no matter the subject matter, freedom's defenses require that critical act first and above all defend the universal right to heresy. For without freedom, the orthodox will slaughter heretics. "Persecution," Mill adds, "has always succeeded, save where the heretics were too strong a party to be effectually persecuted" (33). If reformers' hopes to effect change by transforming consciousness cannot guarantee freedom, then by Mill's logic, reform, lacking self-knowledge of its dependence upon self-negating criticism, cannot but align itself with the power it hopes to reform. This notion puts us in mind, for example, of Said's oft-repeated claim that were the Palestinians to achieve statehood, he would have become their most vociferous critic — because he valued criticism above all other virtues.

We must internalize, too, Mill's sensitivity to the realities of death and physical assault on the heretical. Marcus Aurelius's error is not merely abstract but horrendous in its death dealing and in its effective destruction of a collective possibility of reorganizing society without violence. The fate of Christianity as such is less interesting than the lesson his error teaches about the universal potential inherent in the emergent, which simultaneously appears to destroy an existing if decadent order while potentially reorganizing it. Most important, his error embodies the pre-modern ahistoricality of thought and species that Vico, Dante, Auerbach, and, I contend, Mill so highly prize. The consequences for human bodies, for human apperception, for the perfectibility of the species are profound. There is nothing in modernity to assure that old errors will not recur. In a remark that foreshadows Foucault in *Discipline and Punish*, Mill writes that while "it is true we no longer put heretics to death," we do make them submit to "penal infliction"; even if we do not manage "to extirpate" our heretics, we persecute heresy by war, law, and opinion. We declare heretics "to be outlaws, excluded from the protection of the tribunals." As such, heretics — those whom we declare to be against us because they are not with us — may be "assaulted with impunity" (34–35). The events of 9/11 and Guantanamo Bay return full force to Mill's warnings.

Just as Mill denies that "truth will out," so he says, "heretical opinions do not perceptibly gain" unless they survive "in those narrow circles of thinking and studious persons among whom they originate" (37). Errancy persecutes with impunity, the very quality that defines the arrogant, self-assured, and sheltered position of the torturer. Impunity's corollary is the suppression of the most narrow circles of thought, of all safe-havens where the otherwise persecuted might survive if not thrive. It would be simplistic to assert that Mill speaks of impunity, heresy, and persecution merely metaphorically or abstractly and generally as ubiquitous qualities of all social practice and organization. It would be equally simplistic to ignore Mill's choice of a term, heresy, essential to religion as a key to his theory of freedom. Heresy is not only an eccentric claim in relation to some authorized position and institution. It is not even foundationally the outlawry of resistance to the Universal Catholic Church.

Etymologically, heresy is a choosing, or as the *OED* puts it, a taking for oneself. We should not assume from all this that Mill is replaying a Miltonic theme of Protestant resistance to Catholicism because Mill gives an example of how even liberal or we say in the United States, "mainstream" Protestantism, practices persecution and enforces orthodoxy. In perhaps the longest footnote in *On Liberty*, Mill explicitly links the worst parts of British national character to the massacres and cruelties required to suppress the Indian Mutiny ("the Sepoy Insurrection") and to "ravings of fanatics and charlatans from the pulpit." Remarkably, Mill goes on to criticize very harshly a Christian minister of state, a member of a liberal government, for reserving liberty to Christians alone! In this note, at least, Mill stands ready to concede to Indians the right to liberty! What angers Mill most, however, is the impunity religion and state provide. "I desire to call attention to the fact, that a man who has been deemed fit to fill a high office in the government of this country, under a liberal Ministry, maintains the doctrine that all who do not believe in the divinity of Christ are beyond the pale of toleration." Mill asks, "Who, after this imbecile display, can indulge the illusion that religious persecution has passed away, never to return?" (36–37 note 1). Protestants, it seems, are no better than Roman Catholics are at guaranteeing one's freedom to take things for oneself.[8] Freedom is the alliance of all those who believe in taking things for oneself. Rather than the impunity of the orthodox, a social-political order that protects the violent, the torturer — Mill imagines a Tocquevillian arrangement of laissez-faire and accountability. Mill's vaunted and much criticized emphasis upon individual rights to act freely as long as the actions harm no one amounts to a social practice that encourages emergence within the free practices of choice and negation. Those two together circumscribe errancy while liberating criticism to deny impunity to persecutors. Emergent orthodoxies then rest upon their own first principle of allowing everyone to take things for themselves.

Marcus Aurelius persecuted Christians with impunity. This is a very interesting fact that sharpens our understanding that allied heretics acquire humility as a virtue necessary to check criticism's growth into or upon power. Heretics and humble folk cannot proceed with or assume impunity. In the Roman Republic and according to Roman Law, impunity was an unavailable haven for liars, persecutors, and torturers. According to the Lex Talionis, a wrongly tortured victim had the right, indeed, the obligation to torture his accuser. The law of retaliation set up an order that denied impunity any position whatever in society. Gradually, however, as the Roman Republic faded into the abyss of empire, the state acquired the right to torture with impunity in the name of the sovereign's safety. In this imperial regime, the most egregious forms of violence, all instances of which were legitimate a priori by the underlying principle, could meet any potential or named threat to sovereign power. Treason opened the haven of impunity. In effect, Marcus Aurelius extended the category of treason to Christians thereby reinforcing impunity and marking it as a principle form of power's claimed right to deracinate others not formed within its own orthodoxy. State or sovereign violence against those who take things for themselves could well appear as justifiable force applied to prevent horrible crimes or misdemeanors. Yet, that very notion suggests the dangerous relation between errancy and power. Circumscribing lawlessness within the rubrics of heresy allows the sovereign power to protect itself from punishment for gross violence and horror. Power sets itself a place that is constitutive of law by an exclusion embodied in its worst errancy. Criticism is will and act but is not correlative with impunity since its politics do not foreclose a space immune to justice and its ethos requires a universal identification of heretics with humility.

"Humility," I admit, is not a key term in Mill. It is not like heresy and heretic, a motif that rings throughout his effort to theorize social relations and intellectual ethics. Yet, Mill's thinking requires the term as the exact name for that value or quality essential to the heretics' alliance. Political and intellectual impunity of the torturing and persecuting kind stands in stark anti-democratic contrast to the leveling similarity of all those who choose for themselves. Humility is the same word as humus, that sort of low earth that invites postmodern critical readers, especially those with a post-Lacanian infection, to call "abject." Humus is, after all, a product of decomposition. Nevertheless, critical humility has about it an air of nobility in the name of which it opposes all that which claims impunity and defends poesis as the basis of human futures, human perfectibility, and human historicality. *On Liberty* appears as one of several ideological defenses of this evolved modern possibility that the species cannot afford to lose or see reversed.

A political world that denies space to heretics formed differently than the ruling if decadent orthodoxy is a problematic potential for modernity. While it seems to be a problem of reversion, something like what Freud once described as the death instinct, a return to inertia, it is rather an active potential within the human and the modern to overturn its own experiments in freedom, choice, and justice. The humus of humility is the ground of heretical alliance, poisoned by impunity's desire to foreclose criticism by its echoing approximation in the form of aesthetic self-fashioning. The sovereign and its intellectuals derive their legitimacy from the right to self-making and, so, the right to self-maintenance. From self-making come the accusation of treason and the assignment of right to the arrest of emergence in the name of (even decadent) order. This structure produces a simulacrum of criticism of the sort that wanders, errant, in its own sublimity — call it, "Marcus Aurelius" — and hence, call its murderous acts, "tragic." In fact, if there is a weakness in Mill's theorizing of some processes it lies in his mistaken assignment of the tragic category to an act without redemptive value. From Lear's fatal foolishness, finally, a new and better world appears. From that of this great Stoic philosopher comes the self-protecting right to inflict pain. Murderous persecution — yet again, perhaps — suppresses the better human possibility of poesis.

If Marcus Aurelius is a murderous failure, despite his favorable historical and social location, and indeed because of the peculiar intensity of his mental life as a Stoic and state intellectual, then we must ask if Mill gives us an alternative example of thinking and education. I have presented Mill's Marcus Aurelius in a light that allows a clear comparison with Bentham, whose worst elements the Emperor shares. This implies that the appropriate historical contrast should be with Mill's Coleridge. In my last lecture, I promised to return to Mill on Coleridge and I would like to conclude this presentation with some comments on that essay.

Mill admits that Bentham and Coleridge, despite all their deep differences, believe that serious thinking and politics must begin with a "philosophy of mind." Bentham and Coleridge's philosophies have no common elements. Mill, true to his basic notion that no mind, no philosophy, no group or individual can monopolize truth with certainty, admits that there are elements of truth in each of their positions and that, together, they form a greater truth than either does. Tellingly, however, Mill insists that no single mind, unless it was of the most uncommon variety, could hold these needed conflicting truths simultaneously. He goes even farther to explain with some clarity that human imperfection not only results in even "the mind of the wiser teacher" misestimating the value of any partial truth but also assuring that ephebes, or heirs, to any partial truth misapply and misunderstand its scope and reach. Theories that move from place to place or from generation to generation produce nothing but more error, each time, if we are fortunate, eliciting a counter-balancing correction.

To this relatively uninteresting historical view of truth and thinking, Coleridge, having read Vico, brings an advance. To the regret of his own English and American heirs, Mill insists that the Continental Europeans were ahead of their British counterparts because, in reaction, they were "concrete and historical . . . poetic," rather than "matter-of-fact and prosaic."[9] Coleridge had carefully read Vico's famous essay on Homer. Bernard Knox, the great translator and scholar of ancient Greek, puts it this way when writing on the history of Homeric scholarship: "the Neapolitan philosopher Giambattista Vico had claimed that the Homeric poems were the creation not of one man but of the whole Greek people."[10] Coleridge represented his first readings of Vico as the discovery of new ideas and of several of his own brilliantly expressed. The scholarly history of Coleridge's indebtedness is difficult but interesting. We do know, however, thanks to the work of the great Vico scholar, M.H. Fisch, that Coleridge, like Knox, recognized that Vico had anticipated the German scholar F.A. Wolf's popular theory of a collective Homer. Fisch cites Coleridge's discovery of Wolf's theory, which he had learned as a young man and taken as his own, in Vico's study of Homer. More important, Fisch shows us that Coleridge had spoken of Vico as doing "Comparative History" and, before Walter Scott and James Fenimore Cooper, "discoursed for more than an hour on his Vichian Homeric theory."[11]

Homer matters much less to our discussion than Mill's notice of the Vichian processes of Comparative History and philology. In part, Mill's Coleridge is a supplement to his own practice of "negative criticism." Throughout *On Liberty*, we read a great deal of approaching the truth, producing complementary "truths," and submitting orthodoxies to "critique." For the moment, I want to use the now common word, "critique," not in its strict philosophical sense as we know it from Kant, but from the easier, colloquial academic sense that talks of "doing a critique" of this or that. Criticism, I will reserve for something more conclusive.

If Mill transcends Bentham, as the essay on Coleridge makes clear, it is because, as we suggested in the last lecture, Bentham had a commitment to method and its resultant "truth" that made him unsympathetic and incapable of knowledge. Indeed, Bentham looks like that Descartes whom Vico laments for his adoption of method and his polemics against language, history, and knowledge. I want to add to this constellation, now, Mill's portrait of Marcus Aurelius in part because as a Stoic he falls within that category of Cartesian predecessors Vico also laments. As important, though, Marcus, like Bentham, goes errant because of his intellectual commitments to truth and method at the expense of not only linguistic, historical, and cultural knowledge, but also the generous attitude toward others' beliefs that merit study and thought. As I suggested earlier today — this is a point I will develop later in discussing Wallace Stevens — Marcus lacks nobility, or better, he cannot credit his opponents with nobility of life choice or thought. As a result, he commits mass murder.

Coleridge, unlike Bentham and Marcus, insists that beliefs that "critique" show to be "false" within the confines of method merit respect and attention for several reasons, chief among which is the discovery of essential elements of the species, of the human, itself, in history. Mill's own hostility to Christian orthodoxies is Coleridgean in that Mill finds it important to account for the errors of Christian life and belief. Christianity provides Mill a chance to study residual forces of inert anti-historicism within the forms of modernity and as potentialities within the nature of humans and within the tensions that define modernized socio-political institutions. In general, according to Mill and in sharp contrast to Bentham and, we should add, Cartesians and Stoics, Coleridge, like Vico, takes great interest in the fact of belief, not in its "falsity."

With Coleridge, on the contrary, the very fact that any doctrine had been believed by thoughtful men, and received by whole nations or generations of mankind, was part of the problem to be solved, was one of the phenomena to be accounted for . . . he considered the long or extensive prevalence of any opinion as a presumption that it was not altogether a fallacy; that to its first authors at least, it was the result of a struggle to express in words something which had a reality to them, though perhaps not to many of those who have since received the doctrine by mere tradition. The long duration of a belief, he thought, is at least proof of an adaptation in it to some portion or other of the human mind; and if, on digging down to the root, we do not find, as is generally the case, some truth, we shall find some natural want or requirement of human nature which the doctrine in question is fitted to satisfy: among which wants the instincts of selfishness and of credulity have a place, but by no means an exclusive one. (120)

If "critique" propounds to something called "truth," over and against which it places "fallacy" as its negative object, then Mill admires a criticism that does not set out from some orientation. Mill brings criticism back to expressing reality. He tells us that something long held is not "altogether a fallacy," which does not mean that it is somehow partially true, or believed to be true, but that it is aside, primarily, the a posteriori intention to "true/false," that method as "critique" deploys as the measure of all its values and devalues. Mill's Coleridgean criticism — I want to call it Coleridge's Vichian criticism — sets out knowing that what it studies is an act of will or its result; that it is or was a struggle — a fact of psychological, social, linguistic, formal, and intentional effort against resistance "to express in words something which had a reality to them." Coleridge, we see in this simple phrase, was a greater artist and critic than Bellow and worked within that same line of critical production and worry to which Auerbach also belonged — as we have seen in his remarks on Woolf. Mill continues by stressing that long belief is no guarantee of truth — nothing could be more obvious — but even if shown by the irresistible rigor of stoical, Cartesian, or Benthamite method to be "false," it retains not only value but interest as a willing effort of the human to express, to win through, and to meet its adaptive needs.

Criticism, to put it simply here, is not critique. Although criticism has a negative moment, violence cast against those orthodoxies and methods that would arrest not only the species' poetic productions but also knowledge of history and society comparatively as human — it supersedes critique by its participation in that poetic process over and against which critique establishes itself as the guardian of truth's order. Vico and Coleridge, to figure or name the struggle, are not Marcus Aurelius or Descartes.

Mill's Coleridge not only reads human cultural production as the evolving poetic creation of human will expressing and inventing to meet its adaptive needs, but also supports the idea that such expressive acts might lead to underlying truth. Since Derrida at least, contemporary criticism has had deep suspicions of the Romantics' and Hegelians' use of organic metaphors to formulate stories of human history as the growth of reason in and as history. Derrida in particular has brilliantly studied the elisions between origins and ends in those Hegelian accounts that metaphysically articulate fraught historical failures of thinking and expression. In this context, I dare that condemnation by bringing Mill's Coleridgean roots into connection with the humus of humility. In neither Coleridge nor Vico does a root function as an arché. Deconstruction's critique of Western grand narratives of origins, displaced substantially by Edward Said's Vichian substitution of beginnings for origins and human will for first cause, does not harm criticism's scholarly and human embrace of expressive efforts, no matter how "originary" they seem — in historical, evolutionary, or psychological terms.

My foray into Mill over these last two weeks has had at least two motives. First, I wanted to suggest how critics might adjust liberalism for purposes more useful and productive than those that its opponents rightly oppose. This is itself important because the achievements of a developed liberal thinking, such as Mill's, when properly compared to other historical figures than those that normally frame his work in scholars' commentaries, could benefit many people. Above it, it would benefit all those for whom liberal institutions — free speech, freedom to experiment with lifestyle, freedom to contradict or to escape the dominant — all those and more, such as secularism, historicism, and comparatism — afford intellectuals space to work and refugees or outlaws places of asylum. If torture has returned to history energetically after September 11th, then border control and the extradition have accompanied it, denying the endangered safety, and enfeebling societies by protecting it from unwelcome persons who carry unwelcome formations and attitudes toward thinking. Second, recent academic criticism has embraced a strong anti-liberal position from both the right and left. Stanley Fish and Walter Benn Michaels stand out in the United States for their ability to entrap liberalism with familiar gestures of critique that seem to leave no alternative but, ironically, the purity of the neo-liberal status quo, the dictates of the market, as our sole reality. If Bellow was already enfeebled, these academics promise our enrichment at the cost of our souls.

Criticism's essential role, I had hoped to suggest, belonged to liberal traditions such as Mill's, entangled as they are with Americanism — via

Tocqueville — and with European comparative historicism. Mill understood that liberal institutions require negative criticism to sustain freedom and critical poetry to enhance the species' adaptive perfection. When we lose sight of these lessons and of the historical figures and texts that embody them or represent them, we then put our histories, our thinking, our futures, and ourselves seriously at risk. We abandon that responsibility that, as Vico and Auerbach show, we inherit from that moment in human poetry and thinking that bears the name of Dante's nobility. When Mill laments that England had become a nation of small things, smaller people, small acts, and that it was typical of its age, of an age of commercial and market dominance, he laments the loss of nobility in thinking and in human will. I hope that my various remarks about humility and Mill's revelations of the limitations of cultural elitism allow me to use this word, nobility, without some conventional and boring charge of aristocratic nostalgia or elitist desire. Vico and the others have a much deeper faith than those who do "critique" in the ubiquitous possibility of nobility in the species' potentials.

Next time, we will extend this discussion with a consideration of two figures, Nietzsche and Foucault, who appear to many readers out of place with Mill or Vico. They do add, though, a great deal to our efforts to understand how many people and many forces fear and hope to destroy what we have been calling poesis. For the moment, we will call their motives by the simple word, "resentment" and try next time to elaborate more of what concerns us by watching the struggles of resentment and poetry.

6
Michel Foucault and the
Critical Care of the Self

The man of *ressentiment* is neither upright nor naïve nor honest and straightforward with himself.
　　　　　　　　　　—Nietzsche, *On the Genealogy of Morals*

If there are relations of power throughout every social field it is because there is freedom everywhere.
　　　　　　　—Foucault, "The ethic of care for the self as a practice of freedom"

Not long before his death in 1984, Michel Foucault gave a wide-ranging interview in which he clarified a number of popular misconceptions about his thinking while calmly describing the work he had before him.[1] The interview is, perhaps, as pedagogical as any Foucault ever gave, setting polemic aside for patient exposition that contains a legitimating of the teacher's rights and responsibilities. We can sketch a rough context for Foucault's remarks. From the late 1970s through the 1980s and perhaps, at least in the United States, onward into the Clinton administration's multiculturalist ideology, the critique of institutions that had begun in and followed the events of 1968 threw into question not only abusive teaching but the very structure of teaching. Commonly, Foucault's critique of institutional power and disciplines converged with Antonio Gramsci's thinking about dominant cultures and cultural politics to dismiss teachers' authority as merely ideology and the practices of power. At times augmented by a particular reading of Paolo Freire's ethnology of the classroom and feminist and minority studies of privilege in schools, this convergence resulted in an often only new-seeming structure best represented by the substitution of a classroom with desks in a circle for the traditional arrangement of lectern and rows of seats. Even the seminar table reorganized itself away from hierarchy.

While this rearrangement reformed especially the humanities' sense of their internal virtue, the university's relations to the state, to corporations, and to society changed in ways many writers have made transparent.[2] Effectively, however, the humanists' commitment to the substitution of circle for lecture drew their eyes away from the external relations of their classrooms and disciplines and, more important perhaps, away from their historical responsibility to the real and to thinking's enactment of that responsibility.

As I have pointed out in previous lectures, during the time of these humanists' reforms there were conservatives or traditionalists who strongly objected. Before we align ourselves too easily with that group, which we might now recognize as the vanguard of recent reactionary formations dominant in large parts of the political, intellectual world, we should remember that their abuses often provoked the reactions they bemoaned. Retelling what the Americans call "the culture wars" between the 1960s radicals and their reactionary opponents — nicely enfigured by the contrast between Clinton and Bush — would take us far afield. Foucault, in 1984, felt obliged to argue that there is no necessary "evil" in teaching. Foucault approaches this moment in the context of refuting an idea his critics attribute to him: "Power is not an evil. Power is strategic games." The game of love is a game "that is not evil," because the relations of power one exercises over another in these games are reversible. Yet, such reversibility is not always a rule in every game and the absence of reversibility does not, by some mechanical gesture, prove those games to be "evil." "We all learn from our students" — a truism beyond denial for all but the rarest of teachers — became within the aura of institutional critique, the denial of legitimacy to games of pedagogy that are, in their moment, necessarily irreversible.

Games of love depend upon a rule of reversibility: "To exercise power over another, in a sort of open strategic game, where things could be reversed." Pedagogical games depend upon a different rule that ideologues misread as repressive: "I don't see," Foucault says, "where evil is in the practice of someone who, in a given game of truth, knowing more than another, tells him what he must do, teaches him, transmits knowledge to him, communicates skills to him" (18). The general purpose of ethics is to avoid the potential for abuse in such a situation, to achieve "the minimum of domination." At this very point Foucault not only contrasts open strategic games of love with teaching, but generalizes from teaching to his most fundamental late insight into the relations among power, politics, and ethics. "I think that in fact," he writes, "there [in the minimum of domination] is the point of articulation of the ethical preoccupation and of the political struggle for the respect of rights, of the critical reflexion against the abusive techniques of government and of the ethical research which allows individual liberty to be founded" (19). In our locale, in teaching, we learn and exemplify the lesson and the tactics needed to achieve this general modern vision that to align simultaneously efforts to speak for ethics and political rights with standing critically against governmental excess so we might create the very bases human liberty requires.

Why do I turn at this point to what might seem a minor text in the history of Western criticism, indeed, in Foucault's own corpus? In part, I hope to continue the exposition we began by looking at Mill but more daringly I want to acquire Foucault for the project of historical humanism despite the fact that scholars most often read his work as both anti-humanistic and anti-historicist. In fact, in *Intellectuals and Power*, I contributed insistently to that reading, which I think we can no longer hold once we have read not only his late texts but also some of his courses at the College du France in the 1970s.[3]

Foucault, as even his opponents concede, did more to alter the work of Western humanistic scholars than any other single figure. His thinking about power, subjectivity, disciplines, discourses, ethics, and institutions influenced general practice and specific radical fields such as gender studies, performance studies, and various areas of genealogical, discourse, and institutional studies. Science studies, for example — the subject of intense debate — depended heavily upon Foucault's path-breaking efforts. Normally, those who came along behind rejected what they took to be the heart of humanistic ideology, that is, the notion that the human subject is stable and self-identical.

In "the ethic of care for the self," Foucault clearly says that the subject "is not a substance; it is a form and this form is not above all or always identical to itself" (10). In essence, this is an ontological claim as much as it is social, psychological, or anthropological. Evidence for the claim appears in Foucault's major studies from the 1960s' examinations of madness. In a commonsense world, his idea has obvious forms: "You do not have towards yourself the same kind of relationships when you constitute yourself as a political subject who goes and votes or speaks up in a meeting, and when you try to fulfill your desires in a sexual relationship" (10). There is, in other words, no underlying uniform foundational subject that regulates self-relation in various contexts of action and desire. In simple terms, we might say there are no defining character but rather varying styles and games of relation in part determined by external rules and expectations within or without the game. Foucault's successors have developed several rewarding research projects based on this way of opening up considerations of the play of the non-identical self. The self appears to be primarily performative and its games regulated socially, naturally, and by complex dimensions of interacting forms of cultural determinants. As a result, scholars have produced a significant number of accounts of human play in these varying contexts, freeing criticism especially to the task of disassembling not only ideological obstructions to lucidity but arrangements of the made-selves for understanding and modification.

Foucault admits that there are undeniable "relationships and interferences" between the differing subjects that play successive or even simultaneous games. These do not, however, form or result from a substantial self outside the transformative processes that above all define and result from human finitude.

Interestingly, however, Foucault's followers have a specific idea of the relation between subjectivity and humanism that is rather narrow. It shows the persistent dominance of what Vico allows us to call the Cartesian paradigm — that which first emerged as a type of thought when the classical Republic of Letters gave way to the Stoics, the cynics, and the skeptics. Even though Foucault is a severe critic of Descartes, historically contextualizing his *Meditations* in such a profound way in his book, *The History of Madness*, Foucault takes Descartes too often as a defining reference point.

I think we can see this and begin to recognize a threat it poses to the extension of historical humanism, from another moment in "the ethic of care for the self" when he elides the subject of knowledge with the practice and ideology of Descartes. I intend to object to Foucault's definitional elision of the Cartesian ambitions for the subject and the category of knowledge. I hope that I convinced you earlier on in my talks that Vico's objections to Descartes's denigration of linguistic and cultural knowledge as unnecessary and unrewarding effectively displaced knowledge with analysis and substituted method for study — all the while, in Vico's eyes, failing to overcome skeptical objections. Foucault makes an interestingly related point in this document, one that should alert critics again to the need for constant historical responsibility to the real (about which I will say more in a minute). Foucault notices that with Descartes what he calls the close classical association between philosophy and spirituality yielded to "an ideal based on scientificity" (14). This is perhaps no more than a truism, one that the great historian of philosophy, Lévy-Bruhl, asserts as a given: "Descartes, believing in the future progress of mankind, considers it to be dependent on the development of the sciences. . . . Thus, although science is not its own end, the fundamental problem of philosophy according to Descartes is finally reduced to the problem of the establishment of science."[4] In his major works, Foucault is nothing if not a historicizer of science who discounts the breadth and depth of its claims to epistemological certainty. Seeing science as a set of games of truth alongside other such games allowed Foucault to create the relations between power and knowledge that for more than two decades now have influenced critical and cultural studies.

Yet I want to propose that we might recognize a problem in Foucault's founding conceptions and so release historical humanism from its fatal alignment with the substantial subject of knowledge. First, however, we should avail ourselves of Foucault's simple explanation of this relation. Classical philosophy, he believes, has the care of the self as its primary concern, not the relations between philosophy and spirituality. His own prejudices gleam through his historical account, that is, he clearly believes we suffer from the loss of that focus, but his work and his attitude are not nostalgic.

There are at least two important points here that support modern criticism. First, from the comparison between ancient and modern, something new emerges and critics must think it as such. Second and this in some opposition to Foucault, the philosophical or Cartesian identification between the subject of knowledge and knowledge must yield to a different sort of historical futural orientation than that Descartes or perhaps Foucault imagines.

Let us take the second first. Among the ancients, "the most important preoccupation of philosophy revolved about the self, the knowledge of the world coming afterwards, and, most of the time, as a support to this care for self" (14). Ethics is the name Foucault gives to this structural mode of philosophy. With Descartes — what Vico calls analysis — the need for certainty and method to assure certainty to ground science displaces the ethics of care for the self from the center of philosophy. We can read Vico, even in his most Ciceronian moment of civic responsibility, as agreeing in part with Foucault on the classical philosophers' ethical preoccupations with the self. This comes clearer in a moment when we realize how broadly Foucault defines the civic consequences of self-care. Foucault and Vico would also agree, I suppose, that Descartes produced or embodied a displacing effect that valorized not merely science but its need for epistemological certainty that the ethical yielded pride of place. As Lévy-Bruhl puts it, "We even observe, in several passages, that the progress of ethics appears to [Descartes] subordinate to that of mechanics and medicine. But these in their turn depend for their advancement upon the establishment of a sound and rigorously demonstrated physical science." In this traditional account, Descartes hoped to build an edifice of certainty, a system of thought that would allow one to "proceed uninterruptedly from the first principles of cognition and of being, in a word, from God, down to the most specific scientific proposition of physiology or of ethics."[5]

Foucault recasts this traditional reading in a most interesting way. He sees Descartes as transferring ancient alignments of philosophy and spirituality to an epistemological ambition that implies ontological and anthropological possibilities for the species. "When you read Descartes," Foucault says, "it is striking to find that in the *Meditations*, there is exactly this same spiritual care to accede to a mode of being where doubt would not be allowed and where finally we would know." Critics take an interest in the assignation between doubtlessness and knowing. Method achieves certainty not only in first principles but extends knowing only as far as its systematicity assures truth. While the Cartesian ambition appears universal in these traditional and radical French accounts, we remember how Descartes himself excluded from his aspirations not only the certain knowledge of what we call linguistic cultural production, but reestablished philosophy precisely by such borders. That Vico, for example, took this to be an impoverishment might appear to some moderns as nostalgia, but he had his own reasons for a comparative study — not only to undermine the pioneering imperial ambitions of such bizarrely exclusionary universalism but also to legitimate linguistic knowledge on the basis of human historicality. The latter is, if you will, the guarantor of what Foucault, resisting nostalgia, admits would be a "new thing," if it emerged.

To complete the discussion, though, of the second point, with which I began, we need only hear Foucault summarize his reading of Descartes to grasp his own repetition of Descartes's acquisition of the subject of knowledge for analytic method. "But in thus defining the mode of being to which philosophy gives access," Foucault concludes, "we notice that this mode of being is entirely determined by knowledge, and it is as access to a knowing subject or to what would qualify the subject as such that philosophy would define itself" (14). I do not propose that we countermand Foucault's interpretation of the history of philosophy. I am more than happy to embrace it as yet another reason to recognize the valued primacy of what we called poesis and criticism in earlier lectures.

Foucault gives us an honorable example. He wants to extend Nietzsche's idea that the first role of philosophy is critique. He brings his work to a near final word on this very point. He speaks of philosophy's "duty" as being "critical in a very broad sense — philosophy is precisely the challenging of all phenomena of domination at whatever level or under whatever form they present themselves." This is an admirable articulation, summing up the motive of a long and influential career. To the degree that normative scholarly or pedagogical practices forget or deny, for whatever reason, this duty, they betray the essential function of not only philosophy but also intellectual life. Foucault, of whom it is so often fashionable to speak as a source of mindless rebellion, aligns himself with no predecessor so much as Socrates: "The critical function of philosophy, up to a certain point, emerges right from the socratic imperative: 'Be concerned with yourself,' i.e., ground yourself in liberty, through the mastery of self" (20). Does it help us to recall Confucius' first saying: "'To learn and then have occasion to practice what have you learned — is this not satisfying?'"

Before I attempt to elaborate the persistent weakness in Foucault's adoption of philosophical critique as essentially the Socratic task of self-making and self-knowing, let me return to the first point I set aside earlier: from the comparison between ancient and modern, something new emerges and has to be thought as such. In keeping with the Vichian insistence that historical humanism requires historical as well as geographical and ethnographic comparative learning, Foucault emphasizes that his own study of past practices and formations might, in comparison with the present, both produce something new and allow its understanding. There is nothing, I believe, in this that Vico would disapprove. Foucault presents the production and understanding of the new, however, because of contact with or among philosophers. It is odd that a thinker of such phenomena as discourses, anonymous knowledge, and so on would choose this sort of subject-centered account of emergence. Of course, this context concerns the ethical question of care for the self so one might expect an account that makes the emergent philosophical subject — the subject of knowledge — a potential reserve for emergence, itself. This possibility is an unfortunate error in Foucault's thinking, one that comes from not superseding the domain of philosophy even in his negative critique of its modern paradigms. Nostalgia is a temptation to which he does not succumb; it defines the philosopher's memory of what history has forgotten as "not very interesting" and unlikely to produce much. Even in this expression of the limit, though, Foucault's concern, as he would say, "to think" the games of truth remains too firmly within a modern philosophical vein, even of critique, to afford much opportunity to develop, as Vico did, the emergent consequences of comparative historicism. "The position of the philosopher," Foucault famously asserts, "is not that of any free man." (13)

What might we conclude? Throughout these lectures, I have posted warnings in several forms against the temptation to philosophy. No one is more aware than I am of the varieties of philosophies, philosophers, modes of philosophizing, and so on that, in their sheer multiplicity, might make nonsense of the warning against philosophy I want to issue to critics. Nevertheless, it should be clear by this point that the philosophy I mean is that which Vico means when he offers his negative criticisms of Stoics, skeptics, and Cartesians alike. In fact, if we consider very briefly some few distinctions between the words "criticism" and "critique" we catch some flavor of the difference I mean.

It is fair to say that "critique" derives its force and prominence from Kant and his traditions, extending in modern Western tradition through both Marxism and formalism. We see it in Adorno and Althusser. More broadly, we see it in the practice of philosophers of science to which Foucault himself belonged — I think of Canguilhem and Bachelard, among others. This school concerned itself deeply with the epistemological possibilities of what could be known or thought. They extended versions of Kant's inquiry into the conditions for the possibility of . . . . While Kant used the term "critique" to investigate the limits of cognition, as it were, others, including Foucault, developed the term's resources to investigate the social, psychological, linguistic, and cultural mechanisms that enable and delimit systems of thought and possibilities of conception, representation, and expression — including performance. All of these, Foucault re-theorized as strategic games, more or less open, more or less based on liberty.

In this context, it makes perfect sense for Foucault to tell the story of thinking and understanding the new as a tale of a philosopher's mind. In his famous speculations on the nature of authorship, Foucault stresses that there are certain authors whose work functions as an origin, that is, as a surplus of potential meaning and textual production and as incomplete texts in need of supplementation in the form of commentary and interpretation. Returning to such figures — Marx, Nietzsche, and Freud are his examples — creates schools of supplementation. The new might result from a contemporary's contact with a past philosopher, but the challenge would be to understand it as new, not as a reaction, a restoration, or even a reformation. This sort of occurrence is so rare, it seems, as to be almost magical. Why? There are deep historical conditions, of course, for the unproductive nature of almost all such engagements. Chief among these is what Foucault designates as nothing less than "the question of the Western world" (15), that is, the question of truth. Foucault has made nothing less than this the subject of his life's work.

In addition, as we see in his work, the dominant question of truth has a double tactical relation to the practice of critique. As in Kant, it not only allows for the re-creation of the project of truth but opens the possibility of its "critical" delimitation, a clear sense of its epistemological and anthropological conditions. In Kant, critique deals with not only a concept and its cognition but also the subject as the condition for thinking that concept. Foucault's developed variations of this tactical move simultaneously allow him to tell a tale in which the history of philosophy as a game of truth modernized as a specific game focused on the new creation, "the subject of knowledge," is constantly available for critique, especially in its seemingly infinite recurring variations and displacements.

We can see the nature of this double tactic in Foucault's elaborations on the game of truth as the Western problem. In 1982, Foucault's contemporary Tzvetan Todorov published a book entitled, *La Conquête de l'Amérique*, which argued that the principle Spanish means for conquering and exterminating populations in Mexico especially were less force of arms and disease and much more the West's adaptive symbolic, logical, and truth-seeking linguistic and cultural systems.[6] Todorov's "critique" of the West's imperium implicated quite powerfully the entire anthropology and epistemology of the so-called "West." Foucault's elaborations belong to the same French effort to think about empire and, by so doing, identify characteristics of Europe that he delimits. So, Foucault goes on to say of "the totality of the game of truth. No doubt that is what has given the West, in relationship to other societies, possibilities of development that we find nowhere else" (17). I submit that this sort of judgment results from that Cartesian tradition that denies the relevance of language and so cannot consider historical cultural processes as poetic practices of freedom and emergence. Not only does it simplify the accounts we need to offer for the horrendous practices of Western extermination, domination, and settlement, but also it effectively denies "the West" much hope for evading the epistemological regime that supposedly defines its identity. The effect of Descartes's influence stares us in the face at this point. Recall the agreement between Foucault and the more traditional scholar, Lévy-Bruhl, on the Cartesian ambition to ground knowing and thinking on the divine certainties reproduced for science in analytic method. Keeping that in mind, we understand perhaps too easily why Foucault finds it so hard to designate an "outside" to the problematic his work reproduces to critique.

Foucault asks the Kantian question for us: what were the conditions for the possibility of the emergence of truth as a defining and inescapable game. "What caused all Western culture to begin to turn around this obligation of truth, which has taken on a variety of different forms?" he asks. "Things being what they are," he continues, "nothing has, up to the present, proved that we could define a strategy exterior to it." What would be the nature of such a proof, we might ask. In brief, it would be a "critical" proof, in the sense of critique, that is, an elaborated demonstration that a claimant to another game did not by the force of internal logic — that often has external forms of power — arrive back, well placed where it began, within the game of truth it hoped to evade or displace. What a demonstration of rigor this would require! Foucault exemplifies the problem. He admits that science — in its broadest Cartesian sense — has had shadow opponents such as ecology "which has often been . . . in hostile relationship with science or at least with a technology guaranteed in terms of truth." "But," he goes on, "ecology also spoke a language of truth," and he goes on to derive from this example the general near if not absolute possibility of departing from the games of truth (15). In essence, the critique of truth repeats the game of truth even as his lucid grasp of the game's universality is itself a form of critique. The potential power of Western culture's reliance on truth is in the possibility of playing within these limits — power over the other, as in the strict case of Mill, because of the fact that only free subjects can speak the truth, not transcendentally, but within "a certain network of practices of power and constraining institutions" (17). If the games of truth contain and depend upon the games of critique — "showing that there [are] other rational possibilities, teaching people what they ignore about their own situation . . . their conditions of work . . . their exploitation" (15) — then no human thought or action stands outside. Mill's insistence on experimental life styles and contested ideas, his and others' profound emphasis upon the value of negative criticism — all this stands arrested within the confines of critique as the pillar of truth's game.

I should add that the late Foucault seems very sympathetic to the ancient Stoic philosophers, especially when he speaks of death and the freedom that approaching life's end provides. Recall, however, Vico's persistent comparison of Stoicism and Cartesianism. Neither tolerated the Republic of Letters; each achieved authority by posing questions of a kind that did not refute but granted authority to skeptics. The bleak severity of Foucault's version of liberty contains a strong motif of Stoicism that allows me to assert its self-defining bid for authority as a romance not with science —- as in Descartes — but with the asceticism of his method's denial of history, language, and culture.

While Foucault clearly distinguishes between the philosopher's responsibility and that of all others, and in such a way as to assign to philosophy a privileged obligation, he also takes the philosopher as a representative figure not only in understanding the dominant Western games of truth but also for the pre-modern or ancient practices of the care for the self. In the second and third volumes of *The History of Sexuality* which do indeed study the care of the self as an emergent, dominant, and declining set of practices and discourses in time, often Foucault offers philosophical reflections as the best expression of the ideals of such practice and their best understanding. In the last materials in his career, the philosophical school he most often invokes is the Stoics' school.

We should recall Mill's pathos-ridden account of the tragedy of Marcus Aurelius when we review Foucault's brief historical statement of the intersection between the ethics of self-care and philosophy. "If you take a whole series of texts," he writes, "going from the first Platonic dialogue up to the major texts of the later Stoics — Epictetus, Marcus Aurelius, etc. — you would see that the theme of *care for the self* has truly permeated all ethical thought" (4). It still astonishes me that such a severe critic of philosophy's history, who thought so powerfully the dangers of disciplinary formation, should not hesitate to assert the evidence of a few philosophical texts as the basis for such a claim on "all ethical thought." Are we to understand that philosophers' work is enough to exemplify all ethical thought? Should we to understand that thought exists only in that domain circumscribed by such series of texts? Alternatively, are we to understand that, like Descartes, Foucault cannot find thinking in those other places that Vico defended against Descartes's anathema?

If we keep in mind Foucault's injunction that there is no value in nostalgia, this interview seems to suggest that Christianity did great damage to the ancient world's combination of ethical thought and practice by reducing the complex civic ideal of care for the self to either a narcissistic sin or a desire for private salvation in an afterlife. After Christianity and Hegelianism established their authority in the West, care for the self "became something somewhat suspect" (4). The West began to denounce the aesthetic, ethical combination involved in self-care "as being a kind of self-love, a kind of egoism or individual interest in contradiction to the care one must show others or to the necessary sacrifice of the self" (4–5). Foucault carefully and thoroughly explains the errors in such normal judgments — following Greek and Roman practice and argument, he tells us that care for liberty circled about the "basic imperative: 'Care for yourself'" (5). Greeks and Romans valued nothing more than freedom in the sense of not being someone else's slave as property or political subject. The most fundamental way to develop and sustain this political liberty was the discipline of self-mastery, of care for the self. As Foucault expresses this ideal, it comes near to sounding like the goal of perfection, but its asceticism is an insufficient basis or "phase" for the emergent historically human to perfect itself. Nonetheless, the ideal of ascetic self-mastery is attractive and a powerful element in the history of subject formation:

> I think that both with the Greeks and the Romans — and especially with the Greeks — in order to behave properly, in order to practice freedom properly, it was necessary to care for the self, both in order to know one's self — and there is the familiar *gnothi seauton* — and to improve one's self, to master the appetites that risk engulfing you. (5)

This late interview is remarkable because Foucault manages so clearly to link his thinking about the ethical subject with his career-long thinking about truth. Indeed, if Foucault is a philosopher of the subject, then this document closes the logic of his project by bringing ethics into relation with truth in such a way that we see the subject as not only in itself the object of thought but as the mechanism for his thinking across all fields that engage him. He develops the link between self-care and self-knowing in a purely classical manner that emphasizes how the educated subject concerned for itself both knows and lives according to the "rules of conduct" necessary for ethical life. These "principles" are, as Foucault emphasizes, "at the same time truths and regulations." The self-caring self-maker must "know" the rules and enact them on him or herself. In this perception, Foucault closes any possible space that might separate knowledge from ethics and ascetic self-making, the aesthetics of self-formation. "To care for self is to fit one's self out with these truths. That is where ethics is linked to the game of truth" (5) and, as we understand, to the games of power.

We note, though, that this formulation precisely brings the problems of ethics back into the domain of philosophy and later the subject of truth. For what is "knowing," even in this pre-modern formation, but knowing the truth? Foucault would not deny this nor believe there is any problem with the assertion. Recall, though, Mill's paradigmatic disappointment with Marcus Aurelius whose remarkable ethical Stoicism he and Foucault both admire. Within the modalities that link self-making to civic virtue to the ideals of truth — within all of this admired care for the self, errancy leads to murderous destruction of both the Christian other and the Roman self.

Foucault rightly aims to remind us of how much Christianity costs the civilization with its self-abnegating but egoistic accounts of life unto death, or better, unto salvation after death. Christians, Foucault finds, have a "desire for death" (9) not shared by classical thinkers or those who practice self-care. Foucault's dualistic categories might emerge from liberalism or lend it some support. Like Mill, Foucault worries that dogmatic religion imposes a single mode of existence — an existence unto salvation rather than an existence unto death — upon all individuals dissipating their desire for liberty in several drainage channels of self-erasure within a version of the redemption narrative. Nevertheless, if there is any way in which secular liberalism does indeed align itself as an ally of historical humanism it involves grasping individual freedom of thinking and culture and life practice as futural for the species. Foucault seemingly believes that the Homeric heroes' aspiration for honor and reputation that will last beyond their own lives is the essential goal of life. We could account for how Foucault's readings of the ancients allow him, perhaps like Plato in *The Republic* or Socrates in *The Apology*, to preserve a reformed ideal of ethical reputation from the epic heroes, but what matters is the ease with which he places an ideal that Achilles or Odysseus expressed within the practices of Stoicism. All of what Foucault says here is part of his contrast with Christianity.

> With the Greeks and the Romans, on the other hand, beginning from the fact that one cares for self in his own life and that the reputation which we will have left behind is the only after-death with which we preoccupy ourselves — care for self can then be entirely centered on one's self, on what one does, on the place one occupies among others. It can be totally centered on the acceptance of death — which will be most evident in later Stoicism — even up to a certain point almost become a desire for death. It can be, at the same time, if not care for others, at least a care for one's self which will be beneficial to others. It is interesting to note in Seneca, for example, the importance of the theme: "let us hasten to grow old, let us hasten to the appointed time which will permit us to rejoin our selves." This sort of moment before death, where nothing more can happen . . . is like a movement to articulate one's existence to the point where there would be nothing else before it but the possibility of death. (9)

Those who know Foucault's work and his influences recognize some of his modern sources in this way of talking. Even though Foucault's research shows that our way of being as opposed to that of the Stoics, for example, is not necessary or natural, his range of reference is narrower than these questions demand. Care for the self alerts others to egoism, but the ahistoricity of such a concept in practice, as Mill began to show in reading Marcus Aurelius's tragic error of genocide and torture, reflects the diminishment of imagination (à la Bellow) and knowledge that Vico warned against in his criticism of analysis as a failed desire for certain knowledge.

An account of Marcus Aurelius's error would require a textured description and rearticulating that could never achieve the certitude that the Cartesian analytic or its posthumous after-effects desire. Criticism cannot meet its obligations to the historical real from within the frame of modern philosophy, even if it makes "critique" the preferred inheritance of that tradition. The frame, once granted its authority, so displaces competitive modalities of mind and work, so simplifies and reduces frames of poetic intellectual reference that it cannot but create the self-fulfilling warnings of circumscription that abound even in this most lucid of post-Kantian thinkers.

Criticism's responsibility to the historically human raises the question about Foucault's sense of history. Certainly, Foucault has helped us understand that the human subject is historical; he says as much and insists this truth is both a fundamental result of his research and a condition of its development. Unlike what in the West we sometimes speak of as the "bourgeois subject," that legacy of nineteenth-century global dominance by certain imperial societies, which philosophers and economists alike often assumed to be a natural product of human being, Foucault's researches denaturalized the subject, dissolving it not only into social constructions but into varieties of games. I assent to the idea that Foucault's topic has usually been the subject and not power and as a necessary corollary the nature of human agency and will. His opponents too easily decided that his theories made impossible what is commonly called "resistance," but that is an error resulting from a misunderstanding of Foucault's theory of power — a topic we have already clarified. More important, though, Foucault's late work on ethics intensified his analyses of the ways that human subjects form themselves as subjects within their own freedom. "I would say that if now I am interested, in fact, in the way in which the subject constitutes himself in an active fashion, by the practices of self, these practices are nevertheless not something that the individual invents by himself." Freedom, we have already seen Foucault say, comes from articulating given rules and practices upon the willful acts of self-formation. This is an exceedingly traditional ethical claim and one that Christians would in fact recognize as congruent with accounts of human freedom as a possibility within God's avowed omniscience and omnipotence. Freedom comes from necessity. For Foucault, that which plays the role of necessity is historical, social, and cultural: "They are patterns that he finds in his culture and which are proposed, suggested and imposed on him by his culture, his society and his social group" (11). As liberal as Foucault sometimes seems to his friends and enemies alike, such ideas about the force of context and the embrace of the given as a necessity of aesthetic self-making come into profound tension with such aspirations for individualized freedom in distinction, in experimental practice and heresy, that we have seen Mill admire and defend. Why this difference?

In part, I believe, because critique such as that which Foucault practices and idealizes resolves itself into the representative paradigm of philosophy and the philosopher, the given of which is the inability to treat culture as philology. What Foucauldian critique lacks is the textured reading of word and act as topical and emergent process of creation and struggle. Foucault's special theoretical brilliance is his revision of the theory of power that frees our thinking from the resistance / repression model of classical politics and psychoanalysis. What this theory rests upon, however, is the invariant subtending relation of power and truth that allows truth games to define not only the field of knowledge but the effective purposes and ends of human action and will. Let us treat the matter topologically for a moment. Consider the shape of competing worlds.

Foucault's theory overcomes the classical dualism, making power extensive with truth and liberty, making domination a problem of power, but astoundingly removing power from the circuitries of absolute domination of the sort we see in torture. This is a counter-intuitive but easily grasped notion. What it does not allow us to see quite so simply, however, is the theory's intolerance of contradiction. The contrast the critic wants to sharpen, especially in light of poetry's dependent relationship to embodied contradiction, is the relation between reversibility and contradiction. In irreversibility there is no power; were there power in torture, there would be contradiction. As always with Foucault, the issue is the subject.

Foucault's thinking comes to a momentary conclusion when he insists that there are "two different positions in the care for self." That of ordinary men is less intense "in degree of zeal for self" than that of the philosopher, and this is because, as we have seen, "the philosopher is not . . . any free man" (13). Marcus Aurelius we understand is a best case of the philosopher who is responsible for not only himself and other citizens but also assumes simultaneously that dreamed Platonic role of caregiver to the Prince, himself. In the collocation of Prince and Philosopher, Marcus Aurelius is a tragic and pathetic figure. His error, however, results not from weaknesses of flaws in exercising self-care, even in its deepest Republican or Ciceronian self. As Mill concedes, the Emperor acted with a fully developed judgment of political and ethical responsibility based not on ignorance of those he repressed but on a false model of proper leadership, proper responsibility, and indeed, proper self-formation. Philosophically, he tolerated no contradiction, pursuing stoical resolutions of conflict and disorder. Foucault seems particularly sympathetic to variations on the Greek and Roman ideal of leadership congruent with the liberty and certainty that self-mastery and aesthetic self-making afford. Socrates is the paradigm and *The Apology*, in which Plato records his death, is the foundational text: "Socrates says in the *Apology*, 'I, I hail everybody, because everybody must occupy himself with himself.' Nevertheless, he immediately adds, 'In doing this, I render the greatest service to the city and rather than punish me, you should reward me more than you reward a winner of the Olympic games'" (13). In Socratic critique, we find an ethics of correction in the service of truth. What we do not find in this element of Plato's teacher is a love of literature's lies, of its languages, of its abilities to produce cultures that cannot withstand the test of critique based on the pursuit of non-contradictory truth. In a word, this disdain for a worldscape marred by contradiction knowingly embodies the ideal equation of truth's pursuit with the highest good. We found this enormously powerful alliance, which Nietzsche especially did much to expose, underlying Foucault's great genealogical initiatives of the 1970s. Because of it, Foucault sometimes misperceives and so misvalues the supple complexity of an emergence that is not "the emergence of order" but the emergence of disorderly potential for futures represented by not only Mill-like experimentation but also literary topoi, the commonplaces in formation of dialectical reason and poetry.

Historical criticism notices that neither Athens nor Rome came out well from their moments of crisis, the killing of Socrates, and the torture of Christians. Athens kills Socrates on the verge of its imperial defeat by Sparta. We know full well that in Western history Marcus Aurelius's decisions made irrevocably violent the relation between empire and faith and so sealed Rome's fate with a legacy that haunts us still. If it seems easy to idealize Socrates in light of his persecutors' political incompetence, it is much harder to decide that Rome would have been better off without a reversion to torture and extermination as policies meant to save itself from dissolution. There are no easy choices in these relations. Sometimes, reversibility is not an adequate category for understanding or even designating the presence or play of power. If Socrates is the paradigm of intellect transcending domination in the honorable liberty of thinking, then Marcus Aurelius is the inverted solution of honorable thinking free to murder and destroy self as well as other. If Socrates offers truth and a new modality to defeated dissolute imperial politics, then Marcus Aurelius offers truth and careful self-making as the defense for his decision to murder and mutilate.

If the traditional play of power/resistance was too rigid to think the true nature of power, then reversibility/irreversibility because Foucault rearticulated it upon the games of truth/power, is also too inflexible to account for the various ways in which humans — perhaps even philosophers — live and create without the controlling example of philosophers' greater status as "free men." Greater virtue for doing criticism of human works results from a philological point of view. An historical humanism knows that contradiction is not a compelling issue only in argument and that suppleness of political and poetic invention allows more generously for the detailed emergence of life forms than the dualisms that pursue the embodiment of truth.

Consider briefly an entirely different culture than either Athens or Rome, one that historians consider no less brilliant and original than either of these. I refer to Al-Andalus, a culture and polity founded on escape from imperial slaughter and a love of language, especially a love of poetry. Al-Andalus was, of course, a great society that flourished in what we now call Spain from the eighth century for nearly a quarter of a millennium. So remarkable was that civilization and its culture that the best general book on its history calls Al-Andalus, *The Ornament of the World*.[7] I mention this remarkable society at the end of this talk to recall Vico's strong contrast between philosophy and philology. Its mere existence challenges Foucault's philosophy-centered narrative of the West and the fact that Al-Andalus was a culture of the book in a way that analysis was not and could not be pinpoints the intolerant consequences of universalizing not a Western narrative of modernization but a specific sub-narrative of Europe's history and practices. To challenge Christianity and religion as Foucault does is a healthy aspect of secular criticism's responsibility to the historically human. To do so within a narrative of "truth-centered" stories of liberty resting on an ethos of aesthetic self-making depends upon a prior gesture of ascesis that bears more than a family resemblance to that great Cartesian desire to make extinct all that belonged to the republic of letters.

When I saw that Al-Andalus was a culture of the book, I allude of course to the Islamic tradition of designating the three great monotheisms as worthy of special consideration because of the presence of revealed written truth at their origins. Moreover, though, I refer to the fact that Al-Andalus was a culture of the book in that it was a culture of the library, of translation, and of philology. Although the Koran is notably called an untranslatable book, Islamic cultures were responsible for preserving the secular knowledges of the Western ancient world through their commitments to translation and archiving. Famously, of course, Abbasid rulers, based in Baghdad, commissioned the collection, preservation, and translation of Greek texts into Arabic and circulated them from the Indus to Cordoba. In Al-Andalus, this initiative contributed in part to the creation of a massive library larger by a factor of ten than any collections in Europe. Yet, Al-Andalus, a state created by the deposed Umayyad dynasty that had dominated Islam from Damascus before being usurped by the Abbasids, embodied a culture and politics of immense tolerance and learning that honored thinking and art in forms as diverse and enriching, as contradictory and distinctive, as any we might know. A very simple narrative of Al-Andalus's decline would acknowledge pressures from the Fatimid or Shiite Berbers from the south and the equally ambitious and sometimes equally religious Christian clans from the north. As with most revolutionary transformations, that which ended the Umayyad rule of Al-Andalus not only destroyed its icons of cultural achievement in architecture, but also singularly censored its large and diverse libraries, asserting an ideological and doctrinal uniformity that spoke very clearly of what it found objectionable in Umayyad culture.

Menocal's fine book, *The Ornament of the World*, makes the point that Umayyad culture embodied as completely as did the Abassids in Baghdad or the nomadic populations before Islam the Arabs' love of their own language. She describes "the rich and varied cultural and intellectual Arabophone universe that was the House of Islam [as] the backdrop for the Umayyad vision." Christians converted in large numbers and became thoroughly Arabized, but Jews, whom the previous rulers had marginalized, flourished and together these converts and Jews "added to the every-day expanding Arabic library in areas ranging from science and philosophy to poetry and Arabic philology." I quote Menocal's strongest point in this context: Philology was "the queen of the sciences in an Arabic tradition in love with its own language."[8] Rather than mathematics (as Gauss suggested) or philosophy (as Descartes certainly imagined), Menocal knowingly identifies a successful culture that took philology as the rule of its knowing and thinking. Recall that Vico defined philology for us as knowing what we know as the result of our minds and our actions. A cultural regime that rests on such a foundation not only knows intuitively and thoroughly that historical humanity is the very being of the human but that a proper culture is neither dogmatic nor obsessed with the principle of non-contradiction, not intent on absorbing life and thinking into games of truth — or their perpetuating-because-belated critique.

Games of truth are not contrapuntal in any of the rich senses we saw with Bach or Dante or Auerbach. Counterpoint is much more interesting and enriching than contradiction and its double, the desire for certainty. Descartes, according to Vico, read a great deal but propounded a method and outlook that legitimated heirs who not only did not but also were antagonistic to the very idea. They did not value the library; they valued the method and the proof.

Menocal's history of Al-Andalus contains lengthy discussions of the importance of libraries in that society and makes clear that its social, religious, and political tolerance paralleled those libraries' varied and expansive holdings. The libraries encouraged an active and varied politics and society and gathered the output of that most effective and flourishing culture. In fine, we might say that Al-Andalus was a philological culture and polity; it was an enactment of the love of language and of books.

> Just as essential to the social and cultural project embodied in those libraries was a series of attitudes about learning of every sort, about the duty to transmit knowledge from one generation to another, and about the interplay between the very different modes of learning that were known to exist — modes that might contradict each other, as faith and reason did, and do now. These sat happily in those libraries, side by side, unafraid of the contradictions, first-rate.[9]

Criticism cannot be afraid of contradictions. It cannot hope to expunge them and be responsible to the real that humans are and create. It cannot become rigid in its intolerance of the side-by-side that enriches presences and promises futures that are possible if unknown and uncertain. Standing in front of uncertainty and contradiction without reaching for reason — that is, as Keats told us, a poetic strength. It requires a quality, a virtue, much greater than that of reversibility, which Foucault enshrined as the place of love and as the opposite of torture. Surely, about torture, Foucault was right: where there is no chance of changing places, there is only such domination as to make the existence of the dominated subject impossible or nearly so. Nevertheless, reversibility is not the opposite of such domination. We need another term for a society or culture that commits itself to games of truth enhanced by power as forms of absolute domination, or that self-understands its play as a game of "power/knowledge"; such a society lacks the love of language.

Menocal looks for and finds a simple word to describe the quality in Umayyad Al-Andalus at its height: "suppleness." She comes on the word when describing the amazing fact that a Jewish Prince, Hasdai ibn Shaprut, could rise to be Vizier or Prime Minister to the Caliph of all Islam. It was possible because "such suppleness was a natural part of the landscape of this time and place."[10] Moreover, its enemies loathed just such suppleness. The great contemporary Christian antagonist of Andalusian success could think of no greater indictment than to write that "They gather immense libraries at great expense."[11] In the early days of its success, Christian conservatives attacked Al-Andalus not for its wealth or tolerance, but for its learning, for its languages and knowledges that satisfied the diverse needs and ambitions of diverse people. And at its end, Berber traditionalists, supported in some part by Fatimid originalists, based in what we call Tunisia, destroyed its libraries for similar reasons. Contradiction's intolerance within games of truth hated the suppleness of philological life.[12]

Once these possibilities arise in history however, they do not disappear from critical minds. William Empson, as we shall see next time, will elaborate this set of possibilities for us in an explicit and detailed thinking about poems, critical writing, and their essential place in the formation and persistence of free human subjects.

7
William Empson and the Mind: Poetry, Torture, and Civilization

I believe literature to be the most valuable tool that humanity has found
in its quest to understand itself.

—Orhan Pamuk[1]

The history of criticism takes William Empson to be brilliant and eccentric.
In 2006, writing in *The New York Review of Books*, John Gross called him "a
prodigy" and reminded us that "He arrived at Magdalene College, Cambridge,
in 1925, with a scholarship in mathematics: his college supervisor regarded him
as one of the best mathematicians he had ever had." Three years later he changed
fields and working with I.A. Richards produced one of the most influential
and admired works of English criticism, *Seven Types of Ambiguity* — a classic
that began its existence as an undergraduate paper. Michael Wood says of it, "I
suppose it still bowls over readers of all ages, and not only on first reading, and
not only because of its cleverness. Speaking for myself, I am bowled over every
time I look at it. It is not just that Empson makes us realize, as I.A. Richards has
said . . . 'how much we ordinary readers may be missing.' He makes us feel we
have never read a book properly in our lives before, or more precisely that we
don't know anything at all about what happens when we read." Wood adds that
this comes down to Empson "seeing clearly what most of us dimly feel about the
word." If Empson is, as Charles Rosen puts it, "the finest critic in our century of
English literature," then we should feel some obligation to study and learn from
his work.

The New Statesman once referred to Adam Phillips as "the best psychotherapist
in Britain and one of our greatest contemporary psychoanalytic thinkers."[2] Of
Empson, Phillips wrote in *The London Review of Books*, "There were two related
things that Empson as a literary critic could not abide. One was submission to

authority, and the other was torment, both the wish to inflict it and the wish to suffer it." This fact as much as any other explains Empson's commitment to biographical and historical reading and criticism. Nothing could be more misleading than to take Empson as a mere practical or new critic, a close-reading pseudo-formalist who works, as Murray Krieger once put it, merely to apologize for the poetics of international high modernism, that is, for the mytho-poetics of T.S. Eliot. Empson felt certain that "language can be used to sustain inattention and sponsor cruelty,"[3] and that it almost always did so whenever minds could not be changed or when leaders wanted minds arrested in an unchanging if quite shallow and dangerous stasis.

John Haffenden, a professor of English at Sheffield, has edited Empson's letters, his previously uncollected essays, and written a monumental two-volume biography — in sum, he has done everything anyone might to keep alive his hero's work and reputation. Frank Kermode (who was born in 1919 and so is only half a generation younger than Empson himself) has reviewed both of Haffenden's volumes and mentioned Empson many times elsewhere, usually informatively. In reviewing the second Haffenden, Kermode lets his readers sense the reasons for his reserve and hesitations about Empson, the man and mind: "It was never easy for Empson to have a civil discussion with anybody who took a deviant view of matters he believed to be much more important than an opponent's feelings."[4] I find myself not valuing decorous conversation or an opponent's feelings as much as Kermode but I understand, as Kermode does, some of what it was about Empson that made him intolerant and sometimes intolerable. The first thing Kermode feels required to admit is that Empson was a generous, warm-hearted, likeable man who "would never have pulled rank." When Empson felt that others held opinions he knew were "dirty or disgusting" he set about correcting them and if the others refused to listen or learn, he took to insulting them, having decided they were dangerous, stupid, boring, or some horrifying combination of those vices. He grew increasingly anti-academic as time passed. Phillips puts it nicely:

> Though Empson was never academic in the hackneyed sense of the word he became progressively more anti-academic as he got older, seeing universities, rather like God, as the enemies of free speech and intelligent opinion: they were places in which the obvious got lost, and conversation was replaced by the contemporary form of omniscience called specialization. "The idea that every question has been settled," Empson writes in an unpublished reply, printed here, to Cleanth Brooks's review of *The Structure of Complex Words*, "if only you go to the right Faculty of your University, and that is why you must never mention it in the wrong one, seems to me merely harmful."

Kermode adds that Empson once "told a Princeton audience what was wrong with the horrible new American academic prose — its 'failure to keep the normal living connection between the written language and the spoken one.'"

For such remarks, some conservative U.S. critics and intellectuals, not bothering to read Empson, use him as they often do Edmund Wilson, to mock contemporary criticism's theoretical interests and particular jargons. Correspondingly, of course, as many of you in this audience can tell, advanced contemporary critics have had little to do with Empson, considering him if at all belated, elitist, part of an old and perhaps fortunately passé gang of lit crit types.

My own sense of things is a little different. It will not surprise you that I think my way better, that is, intellectually and imaginatively more valuable, especially if we want to have ways to think about having a future or to imagine those futures themselves.

I think it is quite easy to understand reactionaries' abuse of Empson. His last published book, *Using Biography* (1985), has a title that just waits for the old guard to continue their indulgent bashing of structuralist and post-structuralist questioning of the author — Barthes, Foucault, etc. *The New Criterion*, for example, published a review of Empson's poems in 2001 that found it "best to follow Empson's practice and be biographical. . . . In the end," the reviewer wrote, "as with all poetry worth the name, the reason we go on reading Empson's is to hear a voice."[5] — but they bash more resentfully those native-grown and so even more dangerous critics who want us to read carefully rather than study author's minds and intentions — the Wimsatts and Beardsleys of the Cold War generation, conservatives who were in fact not conservative enough. These conservatives abound in academe and in the public press. We should recall such scholars as M.H. Abrams and Alan Wolfe.

Scholars who are more progressive probably do not take Empson as a particularly valuable resource much these days. In this decade, the Modern Language Association of America bibliographs only 12 items dealing with Empson, including Haffenden; one article published in Tokyo and another in Wuhan, China; a few that refer to Empson's controversial work on Milton; and one article, "Empson's Pregnancy," that alone wants to place Empson within contemporary debates. Despite or perhaps because of some acknowledged relation between Paul de Man and Empson, there is no theoretical treatment that I can find of Empson in the journal literature in some time.

It is unfortunate that Empson has nearly disappeared among English language academics. He is not only an interesting figure in the history of criticism but a critic whose intellectual passions and attitudes might be useful precisely because of his insistence on critics' obligations to the topoi of spoken language and criticism's relations with other prose that accepts those obligations.

When I say that Empson interests us in terms of the history of criticism I do not refer only to a closed story of literary analysis that itself might have an institutional or seemingly autonomous history or narrative. I mean rather that Empson's work responded more to the broad historical world that was his own context and so illuminated our history more than even his most sympathetic readers say. Time does not allow us to detail all parts of this story. Haffenden's biography is an essential tool for such an effort but not quite adequate because Haffenden does not spend enough time placing Empson within some of the more mediated contexts of his time. Haffenden's chapters on Empson in China are remarkably detailed and essential reading, but his discussions of Empson's anger at the Christian God and what Empson called "neo-Christian" criticism dishonors Empson's responsiveness to pressing historical questions.

Empson published *Milton's God* in 1961. His basic reading of *Paradise Lost* is well-known, easily caricatured, and dismissed or ignored. David Mikics has recently studied some of the scholarly relationships and competitions within Milton studies with an eye on the inescapable question of authority. He notes that Stanley Fish departs from Empson at the very moment when Empson stands against cruelty and religion: "Fish backs Empson's view of Milton's God as a sadist. It's just that Fish, unlike Empson, heartily identifies with this disagreeable deity."[6] Fish, of course, continues a very long tradition that embraces Milton's authoritarian rather than a loving Jesus and an ethic of caritas. This tradition has served conservatives and statists very well over time — despite Milton's avowedly revolutionary practice. Why Empson does not want to serve this God or this tradition has one answer in Haffenden's account of his personal history. I want to suggest another by taking seriously and as a somewhat independent process or fact Empson's deep study of poetry. I want to suggest something of why poetry appeals to Empson against cruelty but also how it becomes the basis of a critical possibility within modernism that the time demands and that has its own resources in an ongoing process of poesis that comparative historical humanism has discovered, instantiated, and served at least since Dante.

I have always found Empson's work congenial, partly because his readings were so smart and partly because there is a romance to his intellectual independence. For example, I could set aside his complicity in Richards's plans for "basic English" because when Richards fled China during the Japanese war, Empson stayed on — having himself left Japan for China — and traveled with the exiled faculty of the Beijing universities, teaching and learning at each step. I also admired Empson because his humanism was not sloppy, affective, emotive, or belletristic. He knew that the human had no independence from language and he showed how this is true as both a species matter and a matter of history. Later on, like many others taken with the developing U.S. academic awareness of the aporia as a technical device and an ethical responsibility, I recalled Empson's explorations of human will's confrontations with indeterminacy of meaning and Richards's errors in asserting aesthetic solutions meant to eliminate human psychological conflicts and obscure cultural gaps. Now, however, I return to Empson precisely because of his intolerance for cruelty that Adam Phillips also recently noted. The motive for this return, what makes these old books echo, is the increased prominence of torture in current U.S. and global consciousness and politics.

Until recently, U.S. intellectuals have not much hesitated to criticize torture, even state torture that implicated American policy and training. American state involvement in torture has a long history. For example, in 1956, Allen Dulles, the director of the CIA, sent J. Edgar Hoover, the notorious director of the FBI, a long memo embodying a "synthesis of majority opinion" on the efficacious relationships between torture and psychological technique of subject control.[7] Scholars, activists, intellectuals, and politicians have since the end of the Second World War worried deeply about U.S. state involvement in torture and assassination and in many cases worked hard to reveal and oppose it. For example, following the Watergate crisis that ended in the resignation of the disgraced President Richard M. Nixon and the abuses of power in his administration and that of his predecessor, Lyndon Johnson, the United States Senate, the higher of the two legislative houses of Congress, formed the Senate Select Committee to Study Governmental Operations with Respect to Intelligence Activities. This committee, named for its chair, Senator Frank Church, issued hundreds of pages of reports based on its investigations into the CIA, the FBI, the military's relationships with oppressive regimes as well as abuses of American civil rights and the human rights of people abroad. For a long while, these investigations enhanced the legitimacy of protestors' objections to state practices that offended the rule of law, human and civil rights, and free and open government. Nonetheless, elements of the state's apparatus continued to do the dirty work of power. Such entities as the so-called "School of the Americas," run by the military to train Latin American militaries and police, continued to produce students who often were anti-democratic in politics and violent in their disdain for law and human rights. Mainstream U.S. politicians worried the potential if not fact of abuse in the school and its renamed successor. In 2005, the American House of Representatives, the lower house of Congress, passed a bill that "Suspends the authority of the Secretary of Defense to operate such an education and training facility until submission of a report containing the results of an investigation in response to violations of human rights to which training at such Institute contributed."[8] This bill has not become law due to opposition in the Senate and, I presume, in the White House.

Since the tragic events of September 11, the administration of President George W. Bush has modified U.S. policy and law to draw finer and finer lines between its own practices of interrogation and incarceration and what international law and opinion call torture.[9] As a result, a horrifyingly large minority of Americans — including intellectuals — accept the need for torture and coercion to defend the state and gain information. Given that President Bush's ruling coalition contains among other elements a disproportionately large number of enthusiastic self-described Christians as well as neo-conservative intellectuals, there is good reason to ask about the relation between religion and torture while thinking about the alliances between newer conservatisms and their political allies, the fundamentalists and the torturers.

My limited point is to remind humanistic intellectuals and especially literary critics that their own traditions contain important elements of resistance to such alignments and coalitions and that these elements are not merely personal or ideological but deeply historical and methodological.[10] That is, literary critics who understand their responsibility to the real within the project of historical humanism do good research showing the civilizational outcomes of pursuing the species-destroying practices of torture and abuse. Although Nietzsche and others have made us aware of the species' deep reliance upon violence to form itself as a moral and aesthetic being through ascetic practices of the priesthood, we neither continue the critique of that truth nor recognize that the species might well have transcended its truth. Criticism can contribute to these projects but uniquely and more importantly to the second. This is why I end these talks with Empson, whose work represents the possibilities of criticism within the nightmarish twentieth century even as we promise to exceed it in brutality.

Let us recall some of the context we need to place Empson's work. He provides us with some of it because his writing is so polemical and he does not hesitate to name those he thought were doing God's business. *Milton's God* opens with a polemical description of neo-Christian readings of *Paradise Lost* that gives special attention to the American contributions to the new legitimacy. Within Milton studies, of course, Empson's principle target is C.S. Lewis, whose faith is a matter of record in the service of which he devoted almost all his considerable abilities. (We should not forget the 2005 movie of *The Chronicles of Narnia*.) Empson's more important target is T.S. Eliot, the notoriously influential American anti-democrat, whose stated alliances with authority were strong enough to contradict the greater insight of his best poetry. At first, this is hard to understand since Eliot was early on an enemy of Milton and only later did the Royalist, Eliot, come to a grudging peace with the regicide, Milton. Of course, Empson's target is Eliot's re-centering of the authoritarian God of the Old Testament as a necessary foundation for human society and poetic, critical imagination. Eliot's adaptation to Milton suited the emerging Cold War conservatism within which Eliot subsumed the aesthetic experimentations of vanguard modernism. Eliot's own commitment to a deeply ironic poetics often disagreeably scratched against his cultural policies, and this irritated and dissatisfied some of Eliot's conservative readers who rightly distrusted irony's willingness to abide within arrested minds.

Empson's distaste for authority and tyranny was not limited to churchly matters; he just as happily opposed the tyrannical certainties of cultural nationalists and orientalists. Adam Phillips contrasts Empson with Leavis (in a way that usefully applies to Saul Bellow as well):

> The reason to read literature, as Empson reiterates in his letters, is that it lets us get to know about intentions different from our own, something that is far more difficult than we usually realize. This is what morality was invented to help us deal with. "It seems to me," he writes to Philip Hobsbaum in 1966, "that the chief function of imaginative literature is to make you realize that other people are very various, many of them quite different from you, with different 'systems of value' as well; but the effect of almost any orthodoxy is to hide this, and pretend that everybody *ought* to be like Homer or Dr. Leavis." One of the most effective ways of creating an orthodoxy, as Leavis at least seems to have known, is to identify an enemy: the pretence that everybody should be like X always involves the assumption that they must hate Y, be as unlike Y as possible.

Phillips and I use terms and attitudes associated with critics such as Edward Said or Gayatri Spivak, but it would be well to keep in mind that these are all parts of the same historical contexts of discourses, states, and power. Recall, for example, those years Empson spent in China during the Japanese war. He had an experience there not entirely unlike one I had myself in Hong Kong. Following a lecture on Freud's *The Future of an Illusion*, a mainland schoolteacher told me that she understood the nature of European arrogance: having created such a god on their own authority, how could Europeans feel less than the master of others, she asked. Empson made use of a similar moment to show the dangerous consequences for the poetic crossing of politics and rhetoric in Eliot's misreading Milton. In his preface, Empson recounts an evening, fleeing the Japanese, at a public event, when he recited Satan's speech to the fallen angels. The Chinese, resisting the Japanese in a horrible war of atrocities, grasped and felt Satan's call for resistance against seemingly almighty power, precisely because their imaginations and humanity were not stifled by Augustinian despair, dogmatic arrest, and the congealing of will into belief that Eliot's reading induced and assumed to be the historical reality of politics and language's relational effect.

The modern American reading of Milton was, indeed, neo-Christian and if anything more severe than Eliot's, despite the central tradition of revolutionary thought and practice in U.S. politics and modern poetics. I use the great Harvard scholar,[11] Douglass Bush, as an example because he epitomizes everything that worries Empson. His writings and scholarship also show how hard ideologues work to make us believe that as Milton goes, so goes not only our values, but also America, and the West itself. Empson knew, perhaps intuitively, that America displaced Europe and evidently England in the power arrangements of geopolitics. By 1961, the Christian Milton is an American Milton. In 1944, Bush had delivered the Messenger Lectures at Cornell on *Paradise Lost in Our Time*.[12] Convinced of the relevance of lectures on poetry and Milton during a time of war, Bush began by invoking Wordsworth's image of Milton as the defender of English freedoms against the risks of Napoleonic tyranny.

> In our halls is hung
> Armoury of the invincible Knights of old:
> We must be free or die, who speak the tongue
> That Shakespeare spake; the faith and morals hold
> Which Milton held.[13]

Unlike Wordsworth, though, Bush knew that the Americans had in essence already won the war, so his anxious call upon Milton was, self-admittedly, to win the post-war. "It is rather doubtful," Bush says, "if we do hold the faith and words which Milton held." Eliot most deeply objected to Milton's regicidal politics, but Bush was smart enough to realize that Eliot's aesthetic objections to Milton — Milton was neither imagistic nor ironic enough — would harm Milton's moral and cultural utility in America. Bush worried that irony could be cosmopolitan, skeptical, it might induce anomie — an important point to which neo-conservative intellectuals will return.[14] Conservatives take irony as a stylistic mark of liberal secularism — a fact that Eliot's own Christianity barely overcame in his best late poems. Therefore, Bush could say that America will lose the peace if it follows liberal critics "by summarily dismissing or denouncing Milton's religious ideas." "Millions of people nowadays," Bush goes on to say, "are anxious lest, having won the war, we fail to achieve lasting peace; it would . . . be calamitous if, possessing such a poet and prophet as Milton, we should show ourselves unworthy of the possession" (3). Of course, Bush does not stand for all the beliefs of all Miltonists during and after the Cold War. The newer criticism, during and after the theory movements, changed the reading of Milton to emphasize matters of concern to women and minorities that make important differences. If, however, we take Stanley Fish, the most important recent incarnation of an authoritarian Milton, as influential, as continuing a line from Bush, then we can see the blunt and dull but thick and extended wall against which Empson hurled the brilliant explosive point of Shelley's independent reading of Satan.

Consider that this authoritarian line shadows not only the horrors of Fascism, Stalinism, Japanese aggression, the often very hot Cold War, and now the "war on terror," as well as the wars of decolonization, struggles for civil and human rights, against racism and sexism — and that serviceable scholars like Bush and Fish embrace the authority upon which their prominence depends. Consider all of this and more, then Empson's gestures, and the lucidity that underlies them become interesting.

What is the content of his lucidity? Often when we speak of lucidity, we mean to describe the qualities or processes of a mind at work. It is what the *OED* defines as "intellectual clearness; transparency of thought or expression." The middle-brow reader or ideologue finds too many twists and turns to agree that Empson's mind is clear or transparent, certainly not in expression — and how can a thought be transparent if the expression is not. Set this aside for just a moment, though, to remember that "lucid" is a quality that first belongs to the object of thought and expression rather than to the thought or expression themselves.

In earlier lectures in this series, I described how Vico valued metaphor as a means of acute perception, a mode of intellectual apprehension and consequent verbal expression enabled for those whose perception the prejudice of analysis, Gnosticism, or other forms of linearity have not disabled. For Vico, metaphor apprehends the lucid as Dante presented so lucidly the newly real historically complex depths of human character: what shines the poetic mind apprehends and creates in its responsibility to the real. In all of that, we might say, the mind possesses lucidity.

In English, two great minds, among others, give us a sense of what this means, of what this is like. The first belongs to Wallace Stevens; the second belongs to Empson. Of course, there are serious differences between these two, differences of expression, of conception, and of judgment. I take them together because I want to stress the necessary and mutually illuminating connections between poesis and criticism. Conservative intellectuals and reactionary academics have a romance with the figure of poet-critic; but ideological violence holds little interest for us anymore. We have seen it too often.

Criticism is itself a form a poesis and discovers this about itself only from poetry. As I showed in earlier lectures in this series, historical humanism or what Erich Auerbach calls aesthetic historism imposes upon literature and criticism an ethical, political, and imaginative responsibility to the real. In this tradition, the real is literary, the product of poetic work like that of Dante, which brought into being the complex modern human subject as historical, as a subject that could and must think and oblige its own historicality. Vico met the challenge of this historicality with a renewal of rhetoric, a restatement of Aristotle's position in the topics on various forms of reason and the value of commonplaces. The work of historical culture takes place not in the realm of truth or apodeisis, but in the realm that Vico understands Aristotle to mean by dialectical reasoning, in the domain of that commonly accepted as true.

At least since Gramsci, modern intellectuals have grown suspicious of the commonplace as a realm of common sense, of determinate ideological pre-formation that we objectify by such clichés as "the dominant culture" or "the ruling hegemony." We might say that such designations emerge from the practice of negative critique or more simply that they form a kind of ground-clearing exercise in counter-formation, easily romanticized as oppositional and empowering.

More interesting and more traditional, however, would be questions about the relation between the common and the real, which is a question about the imagination and reality, about the relative responsibility of criticism to poesis as the creation of history. Wallace Stevens opens "The Noble Rider and the Sound of Words"[15] by recalling Plato's *Phaedrus*, the figure of the soul as "of a composite nature — a pair of winged horses and a charioteer" (643). Of course, he intends to think about the same problem as Plato, what we might call the relation between the animate and inanimate, especially of the former's care for the latter. Immediately, however, Stevens deflates the reader, enfiguring the experience of Plato's text as so conditioned by modern history as to be complete nonsense: "we recognize what Coleridge called Plato's dear, gorgeous nonsense" (643). It takes Stevens the entire lecture to redeem Plato's figure — if he does.

Nevertheless, Stevens has identified his approach to the problem of Plato and Plato's problem. In effect, Stevens admits that history makes Plato's figure unworkable: "suddenly we remember . . . that the soul no longer exists and we droop in our flight and at last settle on the solid ground. The figure becomes antiquated and rustic" (643). What has happened here? Simply, Stevens enjoys hoisting Plato on his own anti-poetic petard. It seems Plato's failure is beyond his control since time passing makes what once was effective mute and disappointing. In Stevens's terms, Plato's imagination lost contact with the real — and ironically the failure sets the reader back on "solid ground," abruptly and disappointingly. This seems to be the result of time passing, but nothing could be further from the truth. Stevens's reader is not just in time, later, coming after long and exhausting usage; rather he comes in a different time, as a different creature. He comes when "the soul no longer exists." He reads when there is experience and this controls reading and the efficacy of imaginative figuration. Plato's figure is airy nothingness precisely because it does not and could not have had an historical human reader as the target of its work. I am not sure what its target might have been. At first, the modern literary reader enjoys the titillation of identifying with the charioteer and driving through the heavens, but the figure cannot sustain or nurture this effect. The problem is not aesthetic failure although it might be a deep problem of relativism.

Stevens finds it quite natural to speak of a reader's experience and then to take it as the vestibule to thinking about how imagination and reality work together, how language creates and circulates in light of and sometimes despite what it once already created as the real. If Stevens finds a way to recover Plato's gorgeous nonsense, it can only be after an excursion through modernity's qualities of historicity and humanity and time's ruptures.

Literary readers, because they know a great deal and are practiced, "feel delight, even if a casual delight" (644) in such figures. Stevens allows that such readers might even be moved, not quite nostalgically, but rather as if they were Echo to Narcissus: "while we are moved by it, we are moved as observers. We recognize it perfectly. We do not realize it" (645). Stevens's most telling phrase for demarcating the modern from the Platonic also seems at first to relegate Plato's figure to the waste bin of history, but as the essay's development will show, also sets the conditions for Stevens's renewal of Plato's poesis. (I cannot develop this last theme here.) "We understand the feeling of it," Stevens writes, "the robust feeling, clearly and fluently communicated. Yet we understand it rather than participate in it" (645). The past holds many minds and traditions for which understanding might be enough. Perhaps Plato himself would settle for understanding as a point of departure for greater thinking. For Stevens, however, understanding is mere understanding, a mark of belatedness perhaps, certainly a mark of historical distance, of a kind worth noting. Participation is a form of experience that defines itself to exclude understanding from within and positions understanding as a weak form of itself, an impoverishment that denies understanding's claim to be experience, to contribute to experience, even to be a part of experience.

There is a clear logic to the movement of Stevens's thinking. History has brought consciousness to awareness that high modernism might mark the limit point of modernity's achievement of the species as historically human. Erich Auerbach thinks about the same question in his famous discussion of Virginia Woolf. He celebrates *To the Lighthouse* for its representation of the interweaving between consciousness and the detail, for its manner of being responsible to the realism that historical humanism since Dante has created in literature. At the very same time, working in a comparative field of historical and geographical reference, he laments that the development of literary and cultural historism contributes to an emerging and coercive leveling of a sort that his contemporary, Hannah Arendt, simultaneously lamented as globalizing Americanism.

After Auerbach, we could read Stevens as reflecting upon the historical circumstances to which literary creativity has brought the historical human; as you recall, his essay is genealogical, tracking the presence and reception of nobility in writing as a path along which to think about the relation between reality, imagination, and time. If Woolf constructs a commonplace of Mrs. Ramsey's mending her son's stocking and infuses it with the values of conscious experience, maintaining the essential relation within literature of human subjectivity and the historically real world, this is possible for the same reasons that make it impossible to realize Plato's image of the charioteer. In effect, Plato's figure cannot be a commonplace for us, because we are historical human subjects and Plato is not. More important, Woolf creates a commonplace because our subjectivity is historically human because of literature's creation of the species in those very terms. It is not that Plato does philosophy, which disqualifies him from the sphere of modern realization. Stevens brings his essay to its first climax by explaining, "The reason why this particular figure has lost its vitality is that, in it, the imagination adheres to what is unreal." Stevens means emphatically that there is no chariot in the sky and that there is no soul. In effect, Plato's figure works neither as realism nor as allegory. The surface reason for this reveals a lot — that Plato is no poet, despite his figurative language, and he is no modern, which is to say that because his writing does not create the historically human that human cannot realize the figure or itself in the figure. "What happened," Stevens concludes, "as we were traversing the whole heaven, is that the imagination lost its power to sustain us. It has the strength of reality or none at all" (645–46).

We do not fail to realize Plato's figure because it is belated in its relation to our historicality. Stevens insists on the perpetually belated nature of imagination in a way that reminds us of Nietzsche's insistence on the perpetuity of modernities: "It is one of the peculiarities of the imagination that it is always at the end of an era" (656). This is because realities succeed themselves and successively apply pressure to the imagination. The poet's task is to abstract him or herself from that pressure enough for imagination to perfect its writing so that poetry might have its "own meaning for reality" (658). In an image that brings Stevens quite close to Auerbach's contemporary statements about Virginia Woolf's greatness, Stevens elaborates on what we know to be the credo of all aesthetic historical humanism. "The subject-matter of poetry is not that 'collection of solid, static objects extended in space' but the life that is lived in the scene that it composes; and so reality is not that external scene but the life that is lived in it. Reality is things as they are" (658).

The historical conditions that made this possible disappeared with the twentieth century's violence and transformations. When the British Empire collapsed, nothing remained to hide the universality of disorder and cruelty. As Stevens says, the Empire was shield for some and target for others, but with the end of empire, a changed reality brought almost inescapable pressure upon poets who, unlike Woolf, no longer assuredly filled the quotidian with the meanings of consciousness and emotion.

> Reality then became violent and so remains. This much ought to be said to make it a little clearer that in speaking of the pressure of reality [upon imagination], I am thinking of life in a state of violence, not physically violent, as yet, for us in America, but physically violent for millions of our friends and for still more millions of our enemies and spiritually violent, it may be said, for everyone alive. (659)

No doubt, we feel the need to adjust this remark to our context and to modify its point of view. It matters for me, however — to recall Empson for a moment — that this is evidence of modernism's deep preoccupation with violence and cruelty as threats not merely to poetry as an aesthetic project in a time of horror — poetry after Auschwitz, as we have made that a cliché. In the context Stevens creates, modern violence and cruelty threaten the species' very achievement of itself as historically human through and within the devices of poetry, of poesis as the ability to create itself within the cultures it creates as the venue and reality of its own emergence. After all, Stevens means reality in a way quite close to Dante's representation in *The Inferno*. Stevens feared that reality's pressure — the life lived among extended things, to echo a famous line in his poetry — would destroy what he called the capacity for contemplation without which poesis itself becomes subservient to the deadly ignorance of violence and cruelty's pressure (654).

Wallace Stevens gives us some idea of what modern poets and their readers, like Empson, thought about the possible fate of poesis and the species in the violent twentieth century. He gives some detail to my claim that Empson learned of the species' possible fate from within poetry and something of the fragility of poesis in the face of violent, cruel, and competing authorities. Moreover, as we will see in a moment, it helped Empson elaborate a reading method and a critical practice that took up the task of defending poesis while using poetry and criticism against the violent cruelty that the species brought upon itself as an obstacle to the perfection emblematized by its poetic creations.

Empson's identification of Milton's God with sadism, cruelty, and torture — he calls him a torture monster — is the easiest way into this part of Empson's thinking, but a more interesting place to learn how to read and how to do criticism in this context is his equally controversial reading of George Herbert's poem, "The Sacrifice." I want to set aside the usual controversies as uninteresting. In a word, Empson reads the final variation of Christ's choral lines, which end every stanza in the poem, as too secular, as too psychological, as in fact, blasphemous. Christ dies saying, "Only let others say, when I am dead, / Never was grief like mine." Empson reads this as an example, not easily produced in English, of the "Oratio Obliqua." Moreover, this opens up two unorthodox ideas or associations that once apprehended never disappear from consciousness in reading, unless of course orthodoxy and dogmatism arrest it. The first idea is bad enough; we could read these lines as Christ implying the purpose of the Church is to recognize his suffering, to "be a sounding-board to his agony." The second idea is beyond scandal, anticipating his 1960s jeremiad against god as a torture monster. According to Empson, we can read these lines as Christ's assurance of revenge: "'Only let there *be* a retribution, only let my torturers say never was grief like theirs, in the day when my agony shall be exceeded'" (228– 29). If there is a conflict between a revengeful Jehovah and a charitable Christ, it disappears in this possibility.

Only a critic reading the entirety of this text could come to these possibilities. As powerful as they are, however, they are not the principle interest Empson finds in the poem or that I find in Empson. All too often, as Michael Wood's remarks indicate, Empson's boldness, brilliance, and polemics attract readers' attention. These superficialities often rest on interesting elements of critical practice and theory. In this case, and I take this as pedagogically instructive as well as theoretically absorbing, Empson's grasp of the lucid has three elements: one organizational, a second thematic or narrative, and a third that is structurally human.

The organizational is commonplace within high modernism as the figures of "complexity" or "concentration." The narrative is, in this case, the recasting of the father/son competition as a sort of oedipal struggle for expiation and control: "in the person of the Christ the supreme act of sin is combined with the supreme act of virtue." Concentration looks here as much like condensation as it does like imagistic complexity. As complexity, however, concentration merges with theme and action so that, as Empson says, "we reach the final contradiction":

> Lo here I hang, charged with a world of sin
> The greater world of the two . . .
>
> as the incomplete Christ; scapegoat and tragic hero, loved because hated; hated because godlike; freeing from torture because tortured; torturing his torturers because all-merciful. . . . Herbert deals in this poem, on the scale and by the methods necessary to it, with the most complicated and deeply-rooted notion of the human mind. (232–33)

With these words, Empson ends his discussion of the seventh type of ambiguity. I think that one reason Empson continues to fascinate readers like Kermode, Wood, and Phillips has to do with his perception that poetry is not only the work of mind but that poesis is the means for dealing with the mind. Dealing with the mind means that the mind must be considered as a unit no matter how multifaceted its beliefs. Richards believed that poetry eliminated contradiction and conflict, resolved civil and psychological strife into a discriminated and discriminatory aesthetic stasis. What Richards did not imagine, given his high moralism, was the difference between mind and its contents, or, in Empson's language, the difference between "forces" and "ideas." Empson thought that his critical readings of ambiguity showed that there are forces holding ideas together, indeed, that forces hide within ideas or, more easily, in words. In effect, Empson aimed to show that the mind has forces to hold ideas or words together — in the context of these lectures, this recalls Vico's adaptation of Aristotle's theory of metaphor — that is, mental forces that structure what Stevens calls

.ssures of the real. He also showed that because poetry managed the mind's ambiguities well enough not to fall into disorder, it could make the mind sufficiently unitary, at least in its schema of apprehension and belief, to control the forces that threatened its identity and coherence: Tension rather than arrest. More to the point, mind and poesis are not alternative or different things, not one before the other. As with Herbert's great poem, poesis is the product of a mind and the producer of mind; it deals with mind, that is, poetry is the instrument of mind's organization, stability, and perfection in tension. "I consider, then, that I have shown by example, in showing the nature of the ambiguity, the nature of the forces that are adequate to hold it together" (235).

Of course, two questions arise: how does Empson do this and what motivates him. *Seven Types* ends with an effort to answer both of these questions directly. In light of modernity's Baconian ambitions and Vichian critiques of the same, it is not surprisingly that Empson places his answer in a topos that he believes allows for the strength of poesis within the dominance of scientific force. First, Empson asserts that analytic reading should find its legitimacy within the commonplace of pride rooted in the power of scientific mechanisms' observational indifference. Empson believes that for his method to work, it must appeal to those modern readers who find "self-esteem" in analysis — "a quality that is at present much respected." He then represents the qualities of mind the analyst requires, or those sympathetic to and capable of benefiting from poetic analysis possess. "They must possess a fair amount of equilibrium or fairly strong defenses; they must have the power first of reaction to a poem sensitively and definitely . . . and then, having fixed the reaction, properly stained, on a slide, they must be able to turn the microscope on to it with a certain indifference and without smudging it with their fingers; they must be able to prevent their new feelings of the same sort of interfering with the process of understanding the original ones . . . and have enough detachment not to mind what their sources of satisfaction turn out to be."

Slightly earlier in this chapter, Empson had described a multifaceted, multidirectional set of cultural forces as having new and disorganizing impact upon the intellect of the time. As usual, he put the issue in terms of poetry:

> In the present state of indecision of the cultured world people do, in fact, hold all the beliefs, however contradictory, that turn up in poetry, in the sense that they are liable to use them all in coming to decisions. It is for reasons of this sort that the habit of reading a wide variety of different sorts of poetry, which has, after all, only recently been contracted by any public as a whole, gives to the act of appreciation a puzzling

complexity, tends to make people less sure of their own minds, and makes it necessary to be able to fall back on some intelligible process of interpretation. (243)

Empson accepts that "To give a reassurance of this kind, indeed, is the main function of criticism" (244), so the question seems to be only what sort of reassurance, and his adoption of the scientific model of analysis seems to answer the need.

Yet Empson deeply distrusts the Baconian model of observational indifference. Of course, historical circumstances legitimate analysis, which is the path to both the needed balance and strength of mind required by exposure to difference. "This quality," Empson writes, "is admired at present because it gives one a certain power of dealing with anything that may turn out to be true; and people have come to feel that may be absolutely anything." Like Stevens, however, Empson knows that the very strength of mind formed by the legitimated practices of modern science and poetic humanism can overcome their necessary complement possibly ending the creative species project of historical humanism. He immediately turns the strength of defended and analytic minds into a form of its own weakness, echoing Vico's turn on Bacon: "I do not say that this power is of unique value; it tends to prevent the sensibility from having its proper irrigating and fertilizing effect upon the person as a whole." At other times, subjectivity would have had an easier time managing its satisfactions, seeing its directions, and working for its future. Empson's ethical realism, however, results in an image that does not resolve our conflicting needs but that recognizes them as a problem and opportunity essential to any civilized hope for the species. "But it is widely and reasonably felt that those people are better able to deal with our present difficulties whose defences are strong enough for them to be able to afford to understand things; nor can I conceal my sympathy with those who want to understand as many things as possible, and to hang those consequences which cannot be foreseen" (250). After describing poesis as metaphor — "the perception of the relations between several such things, but then it is the relations which are known poetically" — he comes to his final point about poetry and criticism enabling lucidity. Well-defended minds doing analytic reading open to a variety of truths and sensibilities will at best eventuate in poetic minds that might meet their responsibilities to reality and imagination. To this achieved mind, Empson writes that "You may know what it will be satisfying to do for the moment; precisely how you are feeling; how to express the thing conceived clearly, but alone, in your mind" (251).

We are prepared to accept the commonplace that Empson is aesthetically opposed to "critical dogma" and to what the modernists called "the scientific world view" (253–55). More important, however, we should, like Empson, accept the historical fact that the well-defended mind while insufficient is necessary if the poetic mind and the cultural historical effects of poesis are to survive. The enemy is all that represented by torture, especially what we now call psychological torture, for its intention to destroy entirely the possibility of a human subjectivity well enough defended to be a mind that can conceive a thing clearly, alone or with another.

The well-entitled series, *The American Empire Project*, recently published a book by Alfred W. McCoy who is a chaired professor of history at the University of Wisconsin, Madison.[16] Time does not allow me to discuss the history or workings of psychological torture from the Italian invention of sleep-deprivation in the century before Dante to DARPA's recent funding of neurological research. Rather I will end with McCoy's summary of what happens in psychological torture to point something of the context of Empson's thinking, to suggest the long parallel history of torture and poetics in modernity, and to suggest that the issues at stake are far broader than many academic discussions suggest.

After tracing the history of CIA policy and practice on torture and after noting that the American government ratified the treaty against torture only after adding the codicil that exempts psychological torture from the prohibition, McCoy describes the aims and effects of American forms of torture such as those seen in the photos from Abu Ghraib. (In addition, I will end with this quotation.)

> Comparing the 1983 Honduran handbook [on torture] with the CIA's original *Kubark* manual reveals [which is online in a censored version], in ten key passages, almost verbatim language for both conceptual design and technical detail. After describing psychological techniques to induce "regression" in the subject, both documents emphasize the elimination of "sensory stimuli" through solitary confinement; both warn that pain inflicted externally, by an interrogator, can actually strengthen a subject's resistance; and both itemize the particular methods that will effect a devastating assault on individual identity — disorienting arrest, isolation, manipulation of time, threats of physical pain or drug injection, and careful staging of the interrogation room. . . . "The purpose of all coercive techniques," [the torture instructor] explains, "is to induce psychological regression in the subject by bringing a superior outside force to bear on his will to resist." As coercion is applied, the subject suffers "a loss of autonomy, a reversion to an earlier behavioral level." (91, 90)

We can approach the end of our project at this point. We confront a horrible circumstance, wherein a great republic commits itself formally to a mode of cruelty that it justifies as a necessary means of self-preservation, thereby changing perhaps irretrievably the qualities it claims to defend. Moreover, though, we can see that Western literary criticism, at least since the start of modernity, has had a project that embodies the species' own capacities to historicize, to emerge, and to perfect itself and that this project must accept the challenge that torture at the heart of democracy poses. In Vico's spirit, we see that philosophy cannot rise to defend this project; only poesis with its responsibilities to the historically real as the expression of human will, creativity, and action can do so.

Consider in light of the CIA's aims to disrupt human subjectivity the competing responses of Empson and Foucault. I have nothing but great admiration for the Frenchman, having written extensively about the values inherent in his post-humanistic ambitions. Empson's humanism, however, in the face of torture, reveals its own power, its deep attachment to the species' existence as historical poesis. As McCoy points out, psychological torture causes regression, forcing the subject back to an earlier stage of development. Torturing, being tortured, effectively regresses the species, in terms of not only value and meaning, but in terms of the existing potentiality of the species' subject forms to achieve the autonomy needed for the sort of emergence toward perfection that Mill and others urge upon us. Note how closely Foucault's thinking about torture tracks that of McCoy and the CIA: in torture, there is no reversibility. The game of torture is no game at all. At this point, oddly, Foucault's thinking about power returns to a traditional one, despite his claims. As we recall, Foucault theorizes that power does not exist in torture because there is nothing game-like about it, because there is no possibility of reversal in torture. This is the traditional position differently voiced. Torture does not want reversibility. Consider that those who torture do so to maintain a dominant position or at least to achieve it. The intent of a torture regime is to prevent the reversibility that would allow the victim to exact revenge, duplicate previous suffering, or impose a new will. The torturer tortures so as never to become a victim.

Regressing the subject, destroying its capacity to be complex within itself, that is the effect of torture in both Foucault and traditional senses. As I showed in the last lecture, Foucault's insistence on reversibility is inseparable from his disciplinary affiliation with the philosophical history that controls his understanding of such terms as knowledge and subject. Empson, by contrast, in his reading of Herbert paradigmatically shows that the human produces in and through poetry a capacity to be human beyond the limits of reversibility and non-contradiction. As Empson says of reading carefully, once a thought or possibility arises, the reader cannot forget it. No matter how much at odds the new idea might be with what seems to be the normal or guiding thought, the reader learns to be the sort of creature, the sort of human subject, that can sustain, that must sustain the nervous pathways that allow these various ideas and associations to flow, entangled or free. Such play, far beyond the determining limits of non-contradiction, more complex and numerous than mere reversibility, performs the subject as changeable, educable, and historical. Suppressing reversibility and destroying autonomy are merely the final steps in erasing the emergent possibilities of poetry.

Those ideas the reader finds in texts, words, and experience — which the reader cannot properly forget — are the poem's creation of and responsibility to the real. Criticism's responsibility to poetry's achievement of the human as such a being is its highest civilizational task. Criticism, by definition of its historical existence, then can never be itself if it suffers the allure of philosophy, of ahistorical disinterest, or professionalized conformism. This at least is the lesson that modern Western criticism has to offer to itself and anyone else who willingly listens and judges. All who listen though must understand that such criticism takes itself seriously enough always to engage in a struggle not merely to survive but to thrive, to guide the human to better political and cultural arrangements, and to embody itself in a range of futures it does its best to measure and enable.

A polity that tortures is a polity that regresses, that debauches, and that abandons conservatism for the radicalism of reversion. Against all of it, criticism sets its alliances with the poetic, with history, and with the best the species has made itself. If it refuses or neglects its responsibilities, then its guilt is great and the consequences immeasurable.

Notes

Preface

1. Edward W. Said, "Reflections on Recent American 'Left' Literary Criticism," *boundary 2*, Vol. 8, No. 1, The Problems of Reading in Contemporary American Criticism: A Symposium. (Autumn, 1979), pp. 11–30.
2. Lindsay Waters has persistently criticized Fish and his followers for adopting what Waters calls "market criticism," for turning to a career professionalism and away from a serious critical engagement either with aesthetic issues or cultural politics. See Waters, *Enemies of Promise* (Chicago: Prickly Paradigm Press, 2000), passim; Waters, "Aesthetics, The Very Idea," *The Chronicle of Higher Education*, December, 2005; and Waters, "Market Criticism," *Context*, 2007.
3. Rather than weigh academic influence abstractly, consult "Google Trends" that shows how in 2007 Stanley Fish searches have at times exceeded those for Edward Said. There are very few non-English language searches for Fish in contrast to Said and searches for Fish are in a higher proportion to those for Said in the United States than elsewhere. Of course, the fact that Fish is an American academic who recently has also become a blogger for *The New York Times* explains much of what these results show. That Said has status outside the United States and among non-English speakers, we should also expect, for complex historical and political reasons. We should keep in mind that Said was a profoundly important American academic whose intellectual, professional, and writerly accomplishments should have placed him outside comparison with Fish. That Fish holds up so well suggests his academic influence is proportionate to his professional normality, for which his role as a person related to legal studies is a buttress visible whenever he derives models for critical professionalism from legal professionalism. Cf. the following URL effective as of October 15, 2007: http://www.google.com/trends?q=%22Stanley+Fish%22%2C+%22Edward+Said%22&ctab=0&geo=all&geor=all&date=all&sort=1.

Chapter 1

1. Cf. *The Biographical Dictionary of the Cardinals of the Roman Catholic Church*, at http://www.fiu.edu/~mirandas/bios1697.htm as of July 26, 2006. Among the Papal interests, which the Spanish King had happily shared, was the Inquisition that had threatened several of Vico's friends.
2. H.P. Adams, *The Life and Writings of Giambattista Vico* (London: George Allen and Unwin Ltd., 1935), pp. 88–91, "A Treatise on Method." Adams in this chapter makes two important

errors. Acknowledging Vico's growing distaste for Cartesian analysis and his preference for poetry, Adams nonetheless ignores the political aspects of Vico's thinking here; he claims nothing had changed in Naples despite a rupture with Spain and he ignores Vico's developed reservations about Bacon as well. I mention this study here since as we will see later, Wallace Stevens takes his Vico from Adams in writing "The Noble Rider and the Sound of Words," his great World War II meditation on poetics and modernity.

3. Vico, *On the Study Methods of Our Time*, trans. Elio Gianturco, ed. Donald Phillip Verene (Ithaca: Cornell University Press, 1990), hereafter referred to in my text by page number as *SM*.

4. Samuel Beckett, "Dante . . . Bruno . Vico . . Joyce," *Samuel Beckett: Poems, Short Fiction, Criticism*, ed. Paul Auster (New York: The Grove Centenary Edition, 2006), Vol. 4, pp. 504–10.

5. "Dante . . . Bruno . Vico . . Joyce," p. 505.

6. Slavoj Žižek, "On Divine Self-Limitation and Revolutionary Love," *Journal of Philosophy & Scripture*, Spring, 2004: http://www.philosophyandscripture.org/Issue1-2/Slavoj_Zizek/slavoj_zizek.html. All citations from this interview refer to this website.

7. Cf. Edward W. Said, "'We' know who 'we' are," *London Review of Books*, October 17, 2002: http://www.lrb.co.uk/v24/n20/said01_.html.

8. See Edward W. Said's objections to Samuel Huntington's "Clash of Civilizations?" in which Said speaks of the need to oppose the alignment between such intellectuals and state power as a "crisis of conscience." "The Clash of Definitions," *Reflections on Exile and Other Essays* (Cambridge, MA: Harvard University Press, 2000), pp. 569–90.

9. Joseph M. Levine, "Giambattista Vico and the Quarrel between the Ancients and the Moderns," *Journal of the History of Ideas*, 51, No. 1, pp. 55–79.

10. *De Nostri Temporis Ratione Dissertation a Joh. Baptista A Vico Neapolitano* (Neapoli: Felicis Mosca, 1709), p. 9.

11. Virgil, *The Aeneid*, Book 4, ll. 119f.

12. *The Aeneid of Virgil*, trans. Allen Mandelbaum (New York: Bantam Books, 1972), p. 85.

13. Henry Adams's so-called pessimism about history stems from the American embrace of this Baconian model within the practices of industrial capital and its centralization in anti-democratic institutions of power. Cf. *The Education of Henry Adams* (New York: The Library of America, 1983), pp. 1153 ff.

14. See Paul de Man, "Literary History and Literary Modernity," *Blindness and Insight* (New York: Oxford University Press, 1971), pp. 142–65.

15. When the *OED* cites Bacon on the use of prospect, it does so tellingly, quoting Bacon using the term as a means to see errors humans have made. From this point of view, as it were, such criticisms of modern enframing as that offered by Heidegger reappear as pioneering efforts in precisely the Baconian sense.

16. See Stanley Fish's extended debate with Edward W. Said in the pages of *Critical Inquiry* — for example, "Profession Despise Thyself: Fear and Self-Loathing in Literary Studies," *CI*, December, 1983, Vol. 10, No. 2 and Said's piece in the same issue: "Response to Stanley Fish." For some evidence of Fish's rather open serving of the status quo, see his effort publicly to narrow the range of academic freedom in a thoroughly conservative and anti-intellectual moment in U.S. history, "Conspiracy Theories 101," *New York Times*, July 23, 2006 Late Edition Section 4, Page 13, Column 1.

17. I have given some example of how this works in my essay, "The Crisis of Editing," *ADE Bulletin*, 131, Spring, 2002, pp. 34–40. As an example of this idea at work, cf. Gerald Graff, *Beyond the Culture Wars: How Teaching the Conflicts Can Revitalize American Education* (New York: W.W. Norton & Co., 1992).

18. Giambattista Vico, *On the Most Ancient Wisdom of the Italians Unearthed from the Origins of the Latin Language*, trans. L.M. Palmer (Ithaca, NY: Cornell University Press, 1988).
19. "Second Response," *On the Most Ancient Wisdom of the Italians*, p. 184.
20. *Beginnings: Intention and Method* (NY: Basic Books, 1975).
21. *On the Most Ancient Wisdom of the Italians*, p. 182.
22. *On the Most Ancient Wisdom of the Italians*, p. 182.
23. *The Complete Works of Aristotle, The Revised Oxford Translation*, ed. Jonathan Barnes (Princeton: Princeton University Press, Bollingen Series LXXI– 2, 1984), *Topics*, trans. W.A. Pickard, Vol. 1, p. 167.
24. *On the Most Ancient Wisdom of the Italians*, p. 182.
25. *On the Most Ancient Wisdom of the Italians*, pp. 182–83.
26. It is here that we would place modern policy experts and game theorists in think tanks and universities.
27. For an introductory discussion of the sorites, see the online *Stanford Encyclopedia of Philosophy* at http://plato.stanford.edu/entries/sorites-paradox/ (as of August 8, 2006).
28. *On the Most Ancient Wisdom of the Italians*, p. 183.

Chapter 2

1. For the U.S. context, see Chalmers Johnson, "Republic or Empire," *Harper's Magazine*, January 2007. See as well the ubiquitous but now discredited best seller, Michael Hardt and Antonio Negri, *Empire* (Cambridge: Harvard University Press, 2000).
2. Take as an example, Carl Boggs, *The End of Politics* (New York: Guilford Press, 1999).
3. From a different context but with a relevant set of "heirs," see J-F Lyotard, *The Inhuman*, trans. Geoffrey Bennington and Rachel Bowlby (Stanford: Stanford University Press, 1992).
4. While Vico's influence on late eighteenth-century thinkers of culture is well-known and Coleridge's interest in his work remarkable and influential, and even though we find Vico in Joyce and Beckett, we must agree that the most recent Vico resurgence dates from the 1960s. See *Giambattista Vico; An International Symposium*, ed. Giorgio Tagliacozzo; Hayden V. White, co-editor. Consulting editors: Isaiah Berlin, Max H. Fisch, [and] Elio Gianturco (Baltimore: The Johns Hopkins University Press, 1969) and Edward W. Said, "Vico, Autodidact and Humanist," *Centennial Review*, 1967, 11, pp. 336–52. Said's work on Vico reaches an early culmination in *Beginnings* (New York: Basic Books, 1975).
5. William Wordsworth, "The Tables Turned," line 28, *Lyrical Ballads and Other Poems, 1797–1800*, ed. James Butler and Karen Green (Ithaca and London: Cornell University Press, 1992), p. 109.
6. Aristotle, *Topics*, p. 167.
7. See Friedrich Nietzsche, *Beyond Good and Evil*, trans. Walter Kaufmann (New York: Vintage Books, 1966), p. 2: "Supposing truth is a woman — what then?" In essence, Jacques Derrida attempts to recast Nietzsche's complex answer to this question with his own multivalent meditation on truth's value. Cf. Jacques Derrida, *Spurs: Nietzsche's Styles/Eperons: Les Styles de Nietzsche*, trans. Barbara Harlow (Chicago: University of Chicago Press, 1979).
8. Vico's translator makes this point obliquely in note 4, p. 9 of *SM*: "Vico's allusion is to the Cartesian *cogito*, by which the certainty of existence is to be found in the depths of the doubting consciousness itself; be it noted that Vico did not believe that Descartes had put to flight, had 'routed' skepticism."

9. Admittedly, there is controversy over the exact nature of Bacon's understanding of the King's notorious use of torture. David Jardine holds that torture was explicitly part of the royal prerogative while John H. Langbein denies it. Langbein does, however, show documentary proof that Bacon was five times "a commissioner to examine under torture." Cf. Jardine, *A Reading On The Use Of Torture In The Criminal Law Of England Previously To The Commonwealth: Delivered At New Inn Hall In Michaelmas Term, 1836, By Appointment Of The Honourable Society Of The Middle Temple* (London: Baldwin and Cradock, 1837) and Langbein, *Torture and the Law of Proof* (Chicago: University of Chicago Press, 1977), p. 129. See also, John Parry, "Finding a Right to be Tortured," *Law and Literature*, 2007, Vol. 19, No. 5, pp. 207–28. Thanks to Professor Penelope Pether for showing me this essay.

10. Quoted in Henry C. Lea, *Superstition and Force: Essays on the Wager of Law — the Wager of Battle — The Ordeal — Torture* (Philadelphia: Collins, Printer, 1866), p. 379.

11. We should distinguish between critique and criticism in a way that the philosopher Raymond Geuss fails to do in his recent book, *Outside Ethics* (Princeton: Princeton University Press, 2005), especially in his ninth and tenth chapters.

12. As quoted from "Einstein's Unfinished Symphony," BBC, http://www.bbc.co.uk/sn/tvradio/programmes/horizon/einstein_symphony_prog_summary.shtml, as of May 17, 2006.

13. Stephen W. Hawking, *A Brief History of Time* (New York: Bantam Books, 1988), p. 193.

14. Edward W. Said, *Beginnings: Intention and Method* (New York: Basic Books, 1975), pp. 83–84.

15. The editors of the Internet Movie Database sum up the film in this way: "Elmer Gantry, salesman, teams up with Sister Sharon Falconer, evangelist, to sell religion to America in the 1920's. They make enough money to build a temple, and Sister Sharon falls for Elmer. Elmer is tested by temptation and almost capitulates, but is then wrongly accused by the jilted temptress. But Sharon stands by her man and truth prevails, until both are seduced by fame and blind faith over common sense, and fate deals them a crushing blow." http://www.imdb.com/title/tt0053793/plotsummary. See forthcoming, Jason Stevens's introduction to the new Signet edition of this classic novel.

16. Suspicion of populist ineloquence abounds as well. A good deal of intellectuals' hostility to George W. Bush rests on his stylistic abuse of verbal eloquence, especially in contrast to his predecessor, William J. Clinton. Cf. Michael Kinsley, "The Limits of Eloquence: Did Bush mean a word of his speech about democracy?" *Slate*, November 13, 2003: "President Bush's recent speech . . . is being heralded as eloquent. Which it is. Some of the finest eloquence that money can buy. . . . The eloquence would be more impressive if there were any reason to suppose that Bush thinks words have meaning." http://www.slate.com/id/2091185/.

17. Longinus, *On the Sublime*, trans. W. Rhys Roberts. http://www.classicpersuasion.org/pw/longinus/desub013.htm.

18. Longinus, *On the Sublime*, trans. W. Rhys Roberts. *Critical Theory Since Plato*, 3rd Edition, ed. Hazard Adams and Leroy Searle (Boston: Thomson/Wadsworth, 2005), p. 95.

19. Longinus, http://www.classicpersuasion.org/pw/longinus/desub001.htm#i3.

20. William Walters Sargant, *Battle for the Mind: A Physiology of Conversion and Brainwashing* (London: Heinemann, 1957). This book has been reprinted as recently as 1997.

21. G. Seaborn Jones, *Treatment or Torture: The Philosophy, Techniques, and Future of Psychodynamics* (London and New York: Tavistock Publications, 1968).

22. Seaborn Jones, p. 244.

23. Seaborn Jones, p. 213.

24. Sargant, p. 282.

25. Sargant, p. 213.

26. See Eric Kandel, *In Search of Memory: The Emergence of a New Science of Mind* (New York: W.W. Norton, 2007), for an account of this science.

Chapter 3

1. Erich Auerbach, *Mimesis: Dargestellte Wirklichkeit in der Abendlandischen Literatur* (Bern: A. Francke AG. Verlag, 1946). In these lectures I cite from *Mimesis: The Representation of Reality in Western Literature*, trans. by Willard R. Trask. *Fiftieth Anniversary Edition*, intro. Edward W. Said (Princeton: Princeton University Press, 2003).
2. *Mimesis*, pp. 174–202. I will hereafter refer to *Mimesis* parenthetically in my text.
3. Christoph Wolff, *Johann Sebastian Bach: The Learned Musician* (New York: W.W. Norton, 2000), hereafter referred to parenthetically in my text.
4. Cf. Jerome Roche, *The Madrigal* (London: Hutchinson, 1972).
5. Karl Marx, *The Eighteenth Brumaire* (New York: International Publishers, 1975), p. 15. There is no translator listed.
6. Dante Alighieri, *The Divine Comedy, Inferno: Text and Commentary*, trans. with commentary, Charles S. Singleton (Princeton: Princeton University Press, 1970), pp. 100–101.

Chapter 4

1. We understand that there are intellectuals of left and right who would dispute Mill's asserted necessity of the primacy of individual freedom. To consider their arguments in any detail is not only beyond the scope of these talks but would represent a critical history of modern political thought and practice. Mill's own writings in defense of the British Empire mar his career and show important limits to the development of his thinking. Postcolonial criticism has revealed the depths of English liberalism's involvement with the Empire and recent criticism reveals the painful irony of a liberalism that determines the value of freedom for white Europeans at the cost of suppression of non-European peoples of color.
2. Indeed, Mill's legitimation of empire was inseparable from a counter-Hegelian desire to bring historicality to the non-white. Abominable as is this practice, it is of one piece with Mill's career ambitions.
3. Some in the audience for previous lectures have asked if "pure literary criticism" is not merely textual explication of meaning and form. To this assumption and other forms of academic disinterested practice, these lectures are refutations that show such questions emerge from habits that are reductive, passive, and anti-humanistic — in a word, ignorant or cynical, but in either case of a sort that puts them on the side of those whom Mill, at least, designates as enemies of freedom and the human.
4. Edward W. Said, *Orientalism* (New York: Pantheon Books, 1978), p. 14, hereafter cited parenthetically in my text.
5. Isaiah Berlin, "John Stuart Mill and the Ends of Life," *Liberty*, ed. Henry Hardy (New York: Oxford University Press, 2002), pp. 218–51; hereafter cited parenthetically in my text.
6. See two recent books that discuss these questions. Linda C. Raeder, *John Stuart Mill and the Religion of Humanity* (Columbia, MO: University of Missouri Press, 2002). Joseph Hamburger, *John Stuart Mill on Liberty and Control* (Princeton: Princeton University Press, 1999). Readers interested in an excellent historical introduction to this question might read Allan D. Megill, "J.S. Mill's Religion of Humanity and the Second Justification for the Writing of *On Liberty*," *Mill and the Moral Character of Liberalism*, ed. Eldon J. Eisenach (University Park, PA: The Pennsylvania State University Press, 1998), pp. 301–16.

7. See Chris Hedges, *American Fascists: The Christian Right and the War on America* (New York: Free Press, 2006), pp. 37–49.
8. Allan Bloom, *The Closing of the American Mind* (New York: Simon and Schuster, 1988). See also, Paul A. Bové, "Intellectual Arrogance and Scholarly Carelessness, or, Why One Can't Read Alan Bloom," *In the Wake of Theory* (Middletown, CT: Wesleyan University Press, 1992).
9. John Stuart Mill, *On Liberty and Other Essays*, ed. John Gray (New York: Oxford University Press, 1998), p. 125; hereafter cited parenthetically in my text.
10. "Coleridge," *The Collected Works of John Stuart Mill*, ed. J.M. Robson (Toronto: University of Toronto Press, 1963–1991), Vol. 10, pp. 119–20.
11. Edward W. Said, *The World, the Text, and the Critic* (Cambridge: Harvard University Press, 1983), p. 13.
12. Eric Stokes, *The English Utilitarians and England* (Oxford: Clarendon Press, 1959).
13. *The World, the Text, and the Critic*, pp. 226–47.
14. A.P. Thornton, *The Imperial Idea and Its Enemies* (London: Macmillan, 1959); reprinted (New York: Anchor Books, 1968), p. 252.
15. J.S. Mill, "Of the Government of Dependencies by a Free State," Chapter 18, *Representative Government*, paragraph 15, originally written in 1862.
16. Note that those American neo-conservatives who argue for imperialism to spread democracy by force do not favor popular democracy at home. For some quick evidence of my contention, see "Without a Doubt," by Ron Suskind: October 17, 2004, *New York Times Magazine*.
17. Richard J. Arneson, "Perfectionism and Politics," *Ethics*, Vol. 111, No. 1, October, 2000, p. 38.
18. Alfonso J. Damico, "What's Wrong with Liberal Perfectionism?" *Polity*, Vol. 29, No. 3, Spring, 1997, pp. 397–98. Damico points out that Rawls has begun to modify his early and influential position. See John Rawls, *Political Liberalism* (New York: Columbia University Press, 1993); these modifications seem to me rather minor.
19. "Top General Explains Remarks on Gays," *The New York Times*, March 14, 2007: http://www.nytimes.com/2007/03/14/washington/14pace.html.
20. See once more the exemplary book by Eric Kandel, *In Search of Memory*.
21. That such figures are still among us, see the recent books by Samuel P. Huntington, *The Clash of Civilizations and the Remaking of World Order* (New York: Simon and Schuster, 1996) and *Who Are We? The Challenges to America's National Identity* (New York: Simon and Schuster, 2004). Cf. also, Edward W. Said, "The Clash of Definitions, on Samuel Huntington," *Reflections on Exile* (Cambridge: Harvard University Press, 2000), pp. 569–90.
22. Cf. Ron Suskind, "Without a Doubt."

Chapter 5

1. Saul Bellow, "FACTS THAT PUT FANCY TO FLIGHT; A Novelist-Critic Discusses the Role of Reality in the Creation of Fiction," *The New York Times*, February 11, 1962, International Economic Survey, p. 218.
2. See Hannah Arendt, *The Origins of Totalitarianism* (New York: Harcourt Brace Jovonavich, new edition, 1973), pp. 474ff.
3. Michael Wood, "Don't You Care?", *LRB*, February 22, 2007, p. 8.
4. See, for example, Paul A. Bové, "A Free, Varied, and Unwasteful Life: I.A. Richards' Speculative Instruments," *Intellectuals in Power* (New York: Columbia University Press, 1986), pp. 39–78.

5. Edward W. Said, *Beginnings: Intention and Method*.
6. The best or worst representative of this attitude is, of course, the American anti-philosopher philosopher and professional anti-liberal liberal pragmatist whose alazonic writings in defense of irony achieve a market success that announces their fitness to the age.
7. See the *OED* entry on aesthetic for a brief etymology and any good history of classical philosophy for clarification.
8. As astonishing at it seems, the current U.S. government is guilty of even worse Protestant repressions than this that outrages Mill. General William G. Boykin, a deputy undersecretary for defense in charge of intelligence, is a fervent evangelical protestant who has "described the fight against Islamic militants as a struggle against Satan and declared that it can be won only 'if we come at them in the name of Jesus.' General Boykin asserted his views in speeches that he delivered in his military uniform at religious functions around the country. In one speech, referring to a Muslim fighter in Somalia, the general said: 'Well, you know what I knew — that my God was bigger than his. I knew that my God was a real God, and his was an idol.'" Cf. *The New York Times*, Bob Herbert, "Shopping for War," December 27, 2004.
9. "Coleridge," *The Collected Works of John Stuart Mill*, Vol. 10, p. 125. Hereinafter cited parenthetically in my text.
10. Bernard Knox, "Introduction," *Homer, The Odyssey*, trans. Robert Fagles (New York: Penguin Classics, 1996), p. 7.
11. M.H. Fisch, "The Coleridges, Dr. Prati, and Vico," *Modern Philology*, Vol. 41, No. 2, November, 1943, pp. 113–14. Fisch's article contains detailed source citations.

Chapter 6

1. "The ethic of care for the self as a practice of freedom," trans. J.D. Gauthier, S.J. *The Final Foucault*, James Bernauer and David Rasmussen (Cambridge: The MIT Press, 1988), pp. 1–20; hereinafter cited parenthetically in my text.
2. The still fundamental text in this discussion is Bill Readings, *The University in Ruins* (Cambridge: Harvard University Press, 1997).
3. As a sign that the attitude toward Foucault and humanism has begun to change, see Richard Wolin, "Foucault the Neohumanist?", *The Chronicle Review*, September 1, 2006: http://chronicle.com/temp/reprint.php?id=k7jgcs3s0cv7rw48sr0hl65xzsnfvl7d. Wolin hopes that by reading Foucault as an ally of the French New Philosophers, he can appropriate him for the moral work of human rights: "The alliance with Kouchner and Glucksmann transformed Foucault into a passionate advocate of humanitarian intervention, or *le droit d'ingérance*: the moral imperative to intervene in the domestic affairs of a nation where human rights are being systematically violated."
4. Lucien Lévy-Bruhl, "Essay on Descartes," *The Meditations and Selections from the Principles of René Descartes*, trans. John Veitch (New York: Open Court, 1968), p. xii.
5. Lévy-Bruhl, "Essay on Descartes," p. xii.
6. Tzvetan Todorov, *La Conquête de l'Amérique* (Paris: Editions du Seuil, 1982).
7. María Rosa Menocal, *The Ornament of the World: How Muslims, Jews, and Christians Created a Culture of Tolerance in Medieval Spain* (New York: Little, Brown and Company, 2002).
8. Menocal, *The Ornament of the World*, p. 87.
9. Menocal, *The Ornament of the World*, p. 35.
10. Menocal, *The Ornament of the World*, p. 80.
11. Alvarus, *The Unmistakable Sign*, trans. and cited in Menocal, p. 75.

12. Today's newspapers express how Al-Andalus echoes in the minds of competitors for real power, ironically without any understanding of the Umayyads' own vision. See "Les terroristes islamistes viseraient les enclaves espagnoles au Maroc," *Le Monde,* April 13, 2007: "Surtout, le mythe d'Al-Andalus — lié à la domination arabe d'une bonne partie de la péninsule entre le VIIIe et le XVe siècle — apparaît de plus en plus comme un argument central pour justifier des attentats sur le sol espagnol. Aux yeux des djihadistes, ce *'territoire perdu'* doit être récupéré, coûte que coûte, au même titre que Jérusalem."

Chapter 7

1. Orhan Pamuk, "My Father's Suitcase: The Nobel Lecture, 2006," trans. Maureen Freely. *The New Yorker,* December 25, 2006 & January 1, 2007, p. 88.
2. The New Statesman Profile — Adam Phillips, *Nicholas Fearn,* published April 23, 2001: http://www.newstatesman.com/200104230011.
3. Adam Phillips, "No Reason for Not Asking," *The London Review of Books,* Vol. 28, No. 15, August 3, 2006.
4. Frank Kermode, "'Disgusting,'" *LRB,* Vol. 28, No. 22, November 16, 2006.
5. Paul Dean, "The Critic as Poet: Empson's Contradictions," *The New Criterion,* October 20, 2001, (2), pp. 23–30. See as well Roger Sale's chapter on Empson in *Modern Heroism: Essays on D.H. Lawrence, William Empson, and J.R.R. Tolkien* (Berkeley: University of California Press, 1973).
6. David Mikics, "Miltonic Marriage and the Challenge to History in *Paradise Lost,*" *Texas Studies in Literature and Language,* Vol. 46, No. 1, Spring, 2004, p. 30.
7. Allen W. Dulles, "MEMORANDUM FOR: The Honorable J. Edgar Hoover, Director, Federal Bureau of Investigation. SUBJECT: Brainwashing," 25 APR 1956, from DECLASSIFIED DOCUMENTS 1984 microfilms under MKULTRA (84) 002258, published by Research Publication Woodbridge, CT 06525. Reproduced at the following URL: http://pw1.netcom.com/~ncoic/brainwsh.htm as of April 2007.
8. H.R. 1217, cf. http://thomas.loc.gov/cgi-bin/bdquery/z?d109:h.r.01217. This is the official website of the U.S. legislature.
9. See *The Torture Papers,* ed. Karen J. Greenberg and Joshua L. Dratel (Cambridge: Cambridge University Press, 2005). This 1249-page-long book "consists of the so-called 'torture memos' and reports that the U. S. government officials wrote to authorize and to document coercive interrogation and torture in Afghanistan, Guantánamo, and Abu Ghraib."
10. Among the many admirable intellectual and political contributions made to this study see as exemplary Page Dubois, *Torture and Truth* (NY: Routledge, 1991) and Marianne Hirsch, "Editor's Column: The First Blow-Torture and Close Reading," *Publications of the Modern, Language Association of America,* March, 2006, 121 (2), pp. 361–70.
11. *A Variorum Commentary On the Poems of John Milton,* ed. Douglas Bush and A.S.P. Woodhouse (New York: Columbia University Press, 1972); Douglas Bush, *John Milton* (New York: Macmillan Publishing Company, 1964); Douglas Bush, *Milton* (New York: Viking Adult, 1949); and Douglas Bush, *The Portable Milton* (New York: Viking Adult, 1969).
12. Douglas Bush, *Paradise Lost in Our Time: Some Comments* (Ithaca: Cornell University Press, 1945).
13. William Wordsworth, "It is not to be thought of," "Poems Dedicated to National Independence and Liberty," *Wordsworth: Poetical Works,* ed. Thomas Hutchinson, revsd. Ernest de Selincourt (New York: Oxford University Press, 1936), p. 244.

14. See Norman Podhoretz, "Henry Adams: The 'Powerless' Intellectual in America," *The Bloody Crossroads: Where Literature and Politics Meet* (New York: Holiday House, 1987). See also Cynthia Ozick's approving review of Podhoretz which identifies his critical alignment of Adams with those "adversarial elitists" making up the New Class of the present age. "Hypnotized by Totalitarian Poesy," *New York Times Book Review*, May 18, 1986; cited from this URL: http://www.nytimes.com/books/99/02/21/specials/podhoretz-bloody.html.

15. Wallace Stevens, "The Noble Rider and the Sound of Words," *The Necessary Angel* in *Stevens: Collected Poetry and Prose*, ed. Frank Kermode and Joan Richardson (New York: Library of America, 1997), hereinafter cited parenthetically in my text.

16. *A Question of Torture: CIA Interrogation from the Cold War to the War on Terror* (New York: Henry Holt and Company, 2006), hereinafter cited parenthetically in my text.

Index

Note: Material from the notes (pp. 137–45) is referenced in this index using the following format: [page]n[chapter#].[note#], such that 137n0.1 would be the first note from the preface, on page 137, and 141.4.2 would be the second note from the fourth chapter, on page 141.

China, 70; American critics in, *xi*, *xii*; Empson
in, 120, 123; One-Country/Two-Systems
policy in, *xi*; rise of, 21
Christianity: Al-Andalus and, 114; Coleridge
on, 92; and death, desire for, 108; ethical
thought and, 107; Foucault on, 108; vs.
humanism, 61; Marcus Aurelius and,
83–85, 89; Mill and, 61, 65, 88, 92–93;
neo-conservative reliance on, 31–32, 61;
self-formation and, 110; state torture and,
35, 122; Žižek and, 4–5
Chronicles of Narnia, The, 123. *See also* Lewis,
C.S.
CIA, 121–22, 134–35
"civilizational inferiority," Mill on, 67
classicists, the, 48
Clement XI, Pope, 1
Cold War, 73, 125
Coleridge, Samuel Taylor: vs. Bentham,
91, 92; on Christianity, 92; Mill on, 62,
80, 91; *Phaedrus* and, 126; on Vichian
comparative history, 91–92
College du France, 99
colonialism: Americanism and, *xii*;
contributions of, *xiii*; of Mill, 65; practical
criticism and, *xii*; Said, Edward, on, *xiii*
Commedia, La. See Dante; *Inferno, The*
Conquête de l'Amérique, La, 105
conservatism, 31–32, 61, 119–20, 122–26. *See
also* neo-conservativism
consumerism, 33, 74. *See also* Americanism
contextualism, deterministic, 45–46
contradiction: Al-Andalus and, 114–15;
vs. counterpoint, 114; Empson and,
136; historical humanism and, 73–75,
112; Keats and, 115; in poetry, 131;
reversibility and, 111
control, mind. *See* mind control
control, political, 34
corporatism, 63; anti-humanism and, 5
counterpoint: Auerbach and, 42–46; in Bach,
43–46; vs. contradiction, 114; criticism
and, 42, 44; in Dante, 42, 53, 55; of Woolf,
53–55
creation, human, 39–41, 48. *See also* self-
making
creativity, 35

"crisis": abuse of, 3; Auerbach and, 7;
etymology of, 3; and language, decay of,
2; pervasiveness of in media, 2; philology
and, 3, 7; Said and, 7
critical analysis, 25, 28, 33; apodeictic
form and, 29; Bacon and, *xvi*; and
contextualism, deterministic, 45–46;
Descartes and, *xvi*, 9, 93; education
and, 14, 24; eloquence and, 29–30; vs.
philology, 26; *Topics* and, 23–24; torture
and, 35, 37; tyranny and, 3, 14, 46;
Wordsworth on, 23; *See also* critique;
philosophy
critical dogma, Empson against, 134
critical situationalism, 81
critical sympathy, 55
criticism: vs. attitudinizing, 79; and
Auerbach, ethics of, 39–56;
authoritarianism and, 67; Beckett and,
3; choice and, 67; contradiction and, 115;
counterpoint and, 42, 44; vs. critique, 25,
93, 104; Dante and, 52; definition of, 24;
eloquence and, 33; Empson and, 117–26,
129–36; error and, 81, 86; essential role
of, 94–95; freedom and, 58, 62; historical
human and, 50; historically real and, 109;
history of, 120; and history, comparative,
68–70; human potential and, *xii*; humility
and, 25; against impunity, 89, 90; and
knowledge, historical, 26; liberalism
and, 74; Mill and, 37, 93; negative. *See*
negative criticism; neuroscience and,
37; Nietzsche and, 25; *On Liberty* and,
importance of, 57–58; orthodoxy and,
66–67; perfection and, 68, 135–36; vs.
philosophy, 23, 69; and play, human,
100; poesis and, *xii*, 126; poetics and, 67;
public status of, 86; "pure," *xii*, 141n4.3;
resistance and, 68; responsibilities of, 44,
46, 50, 56, 136; role of, 62; self-knowledge
and, 28; simulacra of, 90; against torture,
xv, 135–36; as training in topoi, 62–63;
Vico's definition of, 26; against violence,
130; as weapon, *xiii*, 80; as will, *xii*, 67,
80, 93
criticism, analytic. *See* critical analysis
criticism, "pure," *xii*, 141n4.3

critique: Adorno and, 104; analytics and, 25; vs. criticism, 25, 93, 104; deconstruction and, 94; God's plan and, 27; lacking humility, 25; language and literature and, 27–28; Marcus Aurelius and, 93; mathematics and, 27; metaphor and, 28; philosophy and, 28; self-knowledge and, 28; skepticism and, 25; Stoicism and, 25; truth and, 25, 93; universalism and, 26

culture as "willed human work," 67

"culture wars," 98

Dante, Alighieri: Auerbach on, 40–44, 46–56; Bach and, 43–46, 47; Catholicism of, 47; counterpoint and, 42, 45–46; criticism and poetry and, 52; drama in, 41; historic position of, 42; human creation and, 48; humanism of, 48; key signature and, 46; Marcus Aurelius and, 88; mixing of styles and, 47–48; musicality of, 42; order of God and, 47; poesis and, 49; poetry and, 50; prospect (*probat*) and, 11; realism of, 50–51, 53, 55; self-creation and, 44; Stevens and, 129; subjectivity of, 55–56; vernacular and, 49, 34; Vico and, 34; Woolf and, 52–55

death, Christian desire for, 108–9

deconstruction, *xiv*, 94

demagoguery, 30–32

de Man, Paul, 80, 119

democracy, 32–33, 135; Christianity and, 61; destruction of, 27, 58; neo-conservatives against, 142n4.16

Democratic Vistas, 11

demonstration, 19, 23, 24. *See also* analysis, critical; critique

De nostri temporis studiorum ratione. See *On the Study Methods of Our Time*

Derrida, Jacques, 94

Descartes, René: authority and, 15–16; Badiou and, 4; and control, political, 34; critical analysis and, *xvi*; critique and, 93; Foucault on, 100; and history, role of, 16; *On the Most Ancient Wisdom of the Italians*, 14; and power, abuse of, 31; and philosophy, role of, 16; prospect (*probat*) and, 11; on reading, 114; tyranny and, 19; vs. Vico, 16, 31, 100; Žižek and, 4–5. *See also* Cartesianism

deterministic contextualism, 45–46

dialectical thinking, 17

Dickens, Charles, *xiii*

disinterest, ahistoricity of, 136

diversity in Al-Andalus, 113–14. *See also* heterogeneity

doubt, 26, 28

dualism, Foucault's defeat of, 110. *See also* apodeisis

Dulles, Allen, 121. *See also* CIA

ecology vs. science, 106

education, 35; Cartesianism and, 31; critical analysis and, 14, 24; eloquence and, 30–33; Foucault and, 97–98; Gnosticism and, 4; in language and literature, 26; metaphor and, 29; orators and, 34; as political formation, 31; reduction and, 28; reform of, 97–98; Stoicism and, 18; and study, aims of, 13; *techné* (training) and, 35; topics and, 24; Vico and, 8, 15, 33

Eichmann in Jerusalem. See under Arendt, Hannah

Einstein, Albert, 27

Eliot, T.S., 123

elitism: eloquence and, 33; limitations of, 95; Said and, 68

Elmer Gantry: charisma in, 31–32; eloquence and, 33; evangelism and, 31–32; synopsis of, 140n2.15

eloquence, 24, 28–36; abuses of, 30–31, 33, 36; *arête* and, 32; Bush, G.W., lacking, 140n2.16; charisma and, 31–32; education and, 30–33; fear of, 33; and formation, human, 31; human as historical and, 33; imperialism and, 30–32; against inertia, 34; love and, 34; neo-conservatives and, 33; physics and, 28; the sublime and, 32; *techné* and, 32; torture and, 35; truth and, 30–32; will and, 34

emergent, the, 68, 88, 104; in Auerbach, 44, 54

empire. *See* imperialism

Empson, William, 117–26, 129–36; abuses of, 119–20; the academy and, 118; on analytic reading, 132–33; Chinese resistance and, 124; criticism and, 119, 122; on cruelty, 120; on Eliot, 123; vs. Fish, 120; vs. Foucault on humanism,

eloquence, 33; irony and, 124; Mill and, 66; political control and, 33–34; state torture and, 122; Strauss and, 61
neo-liberalism, 60
neuroscience: cognition and, 35–37; criticism and, 37; "a good man" and, 37; as mind control, 36–37; Sargant and, 36–37; torture and, 35–36, 37; tyranny and, 37
New Philosophers, 143n6.3
New Science, The (1744), 2. *See also* Vico, Giambattista
Nietzsche, Friedrich: criticism and, 25; Mill and, 80; *On the Genealogy of Morals*, 97; on philosophy and critique, 102; Socratic critique and, 112; truth-discourse and, 18; Vico and, 18; on violence, 122
Nixon, Richard M., 121
nobility, loss of, 95
"The Noble Rider and the Sound of Words," 126. *See also* Stevens, Wallace
nohta (immaterial things), vs. *aisqhta* (material things), 86
novel, the, 52–53

Oedipus vs. Marcus Aurelius, 82
"On Divine Self-Limitation and Revolutionary Love," 4–5
On the Genealogy of Morals, 97. *See also* Nietzsche, Friedrich
On Liberty, 57–95. *See also* Mill, John Stuart
On the Most Ancient Wisdom of the Italians, 14, 26. *See also* Descartes, René
On the Study Methods of Our Time (1708), 5–13, 19; center of, 23; introduction to, 1–2; as model for critical thought, 2. *See also* Vico, Giambattista
"Oratio obliqua" in "The Sacrifice," 130–31
orators, influence and role of, 34
Orientalism, xiii, 59. *See also* Said, Edward
Ornament of the World, The, 113. *See also* Al-Andalus
orthodoxy: Empson on, 123–26; vs. freedom, 89; impunity of, 89; threat from, 66–67
Outside Ethics, 140n2.11
Ozick, Cynthia, 144n7.14

Paine, Thomas, 36
Paradise Lost, 11; Empson on, 120, 122; Fish on, 120, 125; neo-Christian reading of, 124; Wordsworth on, 124
Paradise Lost in Our Time, 124
parataxis, 41–42
participation vs. understanding, 128
Pater, Walter, on self-making, 80
Peloponnesian Wars, The, and decay of language, 3
perfection: analytic philosophers on, 69; Baconian ambition and, 7; Bellow and, 79; Cartesianism on, 69; criticism and, 72, 135–36; dangers of, 22; the emergent and, 68; importance of, 72; liberalism and, 69; Marcus Aurelius and, 88; Mill and, 69, 71, 79; patterns of, 26; Rawls, John, on, 69; self-mastery and, 107; the sublime and, 32; Vico and, 22, 35
perfectionism. *See* perfection
persecution: of Auerbach, 39; of heretics, Mill on, 87; religious, 89, 143n5.8
personality control, 35–37. *See also* neuroscience
Peste, La, 3
Phaedrus, 126–29. *See also* Plato; Stevens, Wallace
Phillips, Adam, on Empson, 117–18, 119, 123
philology: Al-Andalus and, 113–15; Auerbach and, 39, 49, 55; as culture, 110; Foucauldian critique and, 110; Mill and, 84; vs. philosophy, 113; suppleness and, 115; Vico on, 3, 7, 26, 114
philosophies, topical, and Stoicism, 17–20
philosophy: ahistoricity of, 71; allure of, 103–4, 136; vs. criticism, 69; critique and, 28; Descartes and, 16; ethics and, 107, 108; defined by Foucault, 101; free speech and, 71; as game of truth, 105; knowledge and, 102; on liberal perfectionism, 69; limits of, 101–3, 109, 135–36; vs. philology, 113; poetics and, 23, 28; probabilities vs. "first principles" in, 16–17; self and, 101; spirituality and, 101; Vico and, 16, 28

philosophy, analytic. *See* critical analysis; philosophy
physics, 28
pioneer (*retegit*), 8–13, 83–85; *Aeneid* and, 8; Bach and, 45; Marcus Aurelius as, 84; vs. prospect (*probat*), 10
Plato: *The Apology*, 111; Euclidian geometry and, 29; *Phaedrus*, 126–29; Vico on, 33–34
play and criticism, 100
pleasure and eloquence, 30
pluralism, liberal, and "research paradigms," 13
Podhoretz, Norman, 144n7.14
poesis: abuse of, by Bush administration, 74–75; Auerbach and, 49; criticism and, *xii*, 126; Dante and, 49; historical humanism and, 112, 135–36; as human creation, 40; reflected in law, 34; as metaphor, 29, 133; mind, in relation to, 132; the real and, 135–36; responsibilities of, 75; Stoicism and, 18; against torture, 135–36; Vico and, 6, 15
poesy. *See* poesis
poetics: choice and, 67; criticism and, 67; liberalism and, 57; philosophy and, 23; Vichian, 22. *See also* poesis
poetry: in Al-Andalus, 113; vs. analytic method, 33; contradiction in, 131; Dante and, 52; as education, measure of, 30; eloquence and, 33; as expression of history, 50; as metaphor, 30; against mind control, 37; Richards on, 131; threatened by violence, 128–36; against torture, *xv*, 23; against violence, 129. *See also* poesis
politics, the end of, 21
postcolonialism, *xii*, 59–60
power: abuse of, 31. *See also* tyranny; in Al-Andalus, 113, 115, 143n6.12; knowledge and, Foucault on, 100; neutrality of, 98; in torture, 135–36
Powers, Richard, 79
Practical Criticism, *xii*
probabilities vs. "first principles," 17
probat (prospect). *See* prospect (*probat*)
professionalism, *xii*, *xiv*, 7, 62
prospect (*probat*), 45, 84; Bacon as, 11, 138n1.15; defined, 8–13; Descartes as, 11; vs. pioneer (*retegit*), 10

Proust, Marcel, 52
psychiatry and torture, 35–36. *See also* neuroscience
psychological regression as torture, 134–35
"pure literary criticism," *xii*, 141n4.3

Quintilian, 32, 37

Raeder, Linda C., 141n4.6
Rawls, John, 60, 69; *Political Liberalism*, 142n4.18
realism: Americanism and, 128; Auerbach and, 50–51, 128; Bellow on, 77–79; in Dante, 50–51, 53, 129; Empson and, 133; European, 77–78; and hell, narratives of, 50–51; historicism and, 78–79; love and, 53; lucidity and, 125; Marcus Aurelius lacking, 85; in Powers, 79; Rembrandt and, 51–52; Stevens and, 128; Woolf and, 54, 128
reasoning, kinds of, 24. *See also* Aristotle; topics
reduction: analysis and, 25, 28; apodeictic form and, 30; Auerbach against, 40; education and, 28; Stoicism and, 18
reform: Christian, 65; educational, 98; Mill on, 87
regression, psychological, as torture, 134–35
relativism, 66
religion: and eloquence, fear of, 33; evangelistic 31–32; Foucault on, 108; Mill on, 61, 108; state torture and, 122
"The Religion of Humanity," 61, 141n4.6
Rembrandt (Harmenszoon van Rijn), 51–52
Renaissance music, 43–44
representation in *Mimesis*, 41
"research paradigms," 1
resistance, 63, 67–68, 110
retegit (pioneer). *See* pioneer (*retegit*)
reversibility: contradiction and, 111; in Foucault, 98, 111–12, 115, 135–36; vs. suppleness, 115; in torture, 135–36
rhetoric, 31–32. *See also* eloquence
Richards, I.A., 117, 131
Rome and torture, legal status of, 89
Rosen, Charles, 117